Because
He First
Loved Us

Because He First Loved Us

HENRY B. EYRING

DESERET
BOOK

Salt Lake City, Utah

Visit us at deseretbook.com

First printing in hardbound 2002
First printing in mass market paperbound 2006

Library of Congress Cataloging-in-Publication Data

Eyring, Henry B., 1933–
    Because He first loved us / Henry B. Eyring.
        p.   cm.
    Includes bibliographical references and index.
    ISBN 1-57008-924-8 (alk. paper) (hardbound)
    ISBN-10 1-59038-637-X (mass market paperbound)
    ISBN-13 978-1-59038-637-8 (mass market paperbound)
    1. Christian life—Mormon authors. I. Title.

BX8656 .E955 2002
248.4'8932—dc21   2002010440

Printed in the United States of America
Banta, Menasha, WI

10   9   8   7   6   5   4   3   2   1

Beloved, let us love one another: for love is of God; and every one that loveth is born of God, and knoweth God. . . .

We love him, because he first loved us. . . .

And this commandment have we from him, That he who loveth God love his brother also.

—1 JOHN 4:7, 19, 21

CONTENTS

BLESSING OTHERS IN LOVE

INTRODUCTION

The first and great commandment is this: "Thou shalt love the Lord thy God with all thy heart, with all thy might, mind, and strength; and in the name of Jesus Christ thou shalt serve him" (D&C 59:5). The restoration of the gospel of Jesus Christ through the Prophet Joseph Smith brought many blessings. For me, none is more precious than a knowledge of the loving nature of our Heavenly Father and of His Son, Jesus Christ. When the Holy Ghost confirms that knowledge to us, our hearts are prepared to keep that first and great commandment.

Keeping the first commandment always leads to keeping the second, because to love the Father and the Son is to serve those They love. In answer to our prayers for guidance, They send the Holy Ghost to tell us how to help others and to feel at least a part of God's love. So in that service, our love of God increases and the keeping of the second great commandment leads us back to the first, in an ascending circle. In time, our very natures change. We are filled with the love of God, which, even in a world with so much misery and despair, brings us happiness and hope.

This book is about that love and that service. My wish for you is that you will find, as I have, happiness and hope in the restored gospel of Jesus Christ and in His service. He is the promised Messiah, the Savior of the world. He lives. He loves us. And He leads His Church, which bears His name. I so testify, in the name of Jesus Christ.

Turning
Our
Hearts

A Life Founded in Light and Truth

One glance at the newspaper or at the television tells us that we live in stormy times. One thought of our families grips our hearts with concern for the forces of error that beat upon them. All of us know that we must build our lives on a solid foundation of truth to be safe. And we are under covenant to be witnesses of truth to others as long as we live. It won't protect them just to have our witness of truth unless they build their lives on it. So there are few questions as important as this one: How does a person build a life founded on truth? It won't surprise you that the answer is simple enough for a child to understand but that applying it is easy only to a person who has the heart of a child.

Jesus Christ answered the question of how to build on a foundation of truth with a story. You not only can remember it, but you can visualize it, especially if you've ever lived on a floodplain or in tornado country.

> Therefore whosoever heareth these sayings of mine, and doeth them, I will liken him unto a wise man, which built his house upon a rock:

From a talk given at a Brigham Young University devotional, 15 August 2000.

And the rain descended, and the floods came, and the winds blew, and beat upon that house; and it fell not: for it was founded upon a rock.

And every one that heareth these sayings of mine, and doeth them not, shall be likened unto a foolish man, which built his house upon the sand:

And the rain descended, and the floods came, and the winds blew, and beat upon that house; and it fell: and great was the fall of it. (Matthew 7:24–27.)

LINE UPON LINE

Obedience to commandments is the way we build a foundation of truth. Here is the way that works, in words so simple that a child could understand: The truth of most worth is to know God our Heavenly Father, His Son, Jesus Christ, and Their plan for us to have eternal life with Them in families. When God communicates that priceless truth to us, He does it by the Spirit of Truth. We have to ask for it in prayer. Then He sends us a small part of that truth by the Spirit. It comes to our hearts and minds. It feels good, like the light from the sun shining through the clouds on a dark day. He sends truth line upon line, like the lines on the page of a book. Each time a line of truth comes to us, we get to choose what we will do about it. If we try hard to do what that truth requires of us, God will send more light and more truth. It will go on, line after line, as long as we choose to obey the truth. That is why the Savior said that the man who obeyed His commandments built on a rock so solid that no storm or flood could hurt his house.

In another place in the scriptures, the Lord described in a beautiful way how that foundation could be built so that we could finally come to know all He knows and become like Him and our Heavenly Father:

"I give unto you these sayings that you may understand and know how to worship, and know what you worship, that you may come unto the Father in my name, and in due time receive of his fulness.

"For if you keep my commandments you shall receive of his fulness, and be glorified in me as I am in the Father; therefore, I say unto you, you shall receive grace for grace" (D&C 93:19–20).

And then a few verses later the Lord says:

And truth is knowledge of things as they are, and as they were, and as they are to come;

And whatsoever is more or less than this is the spirit of that wicked one who was a liar from the beginning.

The Spirit of truth is of God. I am the Spirit of truth, and John bore record of me, saying: He received a fulness of truth, yea, even of all truth;

And no man receiveth a fulness unless he keepeth his commandments.

He that keepeth his commandments receiveth truth and light, until he is glorified in truth and knoweth all things. (D&C 93:24–28.)

Here is President Joseph F. Smith's description of the work it takes to build an imperishable foundation of truth: "The men and the women who are honest before God, who humbly plod along, doing their duty, paying their tithing, and exercising that pure religion and undefiled before God and the Father, which is to visit the fatherless and the widows in their afflictions and to keep oneself unspotted from the world, and who help look after the poor; and who honor the holy Priesthood, who do not run into excesses, who are prayerful in their families, and who acknowledge the Lord in their hearts, they will build up a foundation that the gates of hell cannot prevail against; and if the floods come and the storms beat upon their house, it shall not fall, for it will be built upon the rock of eternal truth" (*Gospel Doctrine*, 12th ed. [Salt Lake City: Deseret Book Co., 1961], 7–8).

President Smith made building on a foundation of truth sound like a long list of things to do. He seems to be describing work. I remember President Ezra Taft Benson saying with a smile about his service, "I love this work. And it is work."

Yet you will notice that the work is simple obedience. It is not complicated things; it is not fancy things or getting great spiritual manifestations. This is work within the abilities of the most humble and the least educated.

It Takes Humility

It sounds so simple to build upon a foundation of truth that you may wonder why everyone doesn't succeed. For one thing, it takes great humility. It's hard to repent, to admit you are wrong on faith alone, before the evidence of a feeling of being forgiven and light comes. But that is the way it has to be. First comes obedience and then come the confirming assurances, the revelation of truth, and the blessing of light.

That is so because God gave us agency, not just as a right but as a necessity. We must choose with our agency to obey in faith that the promised blessing will come, that the promise is true because it comes from God. You remember the words of the scripture in Ether, the twelfth chapter, which tell us both why that is hard and why it is necessary:

> Wherefore, whoso believeth in God might with surety hope for a better world, yea, even a place at the right hand of God, which hope cometh of faith, maketh an anchor to the souls of men, which would make them sure and steadfast, always abounding in good works, being led to glorify God.
>
> And it came to pass that Ether did prophesy great and marvelous things unto the people, which they did not believe, because they saw them not.
>
> And now, I, Moroni, would speak somewhat concerning these things; I would show unto the world that faith is things which are hoped for and not seen; wherefore, dispute not because ye see not, for ye receive no witness until after the trial of your faith. (Ether 12:4–6.)

There is another reason why it is not easy for the proud to build on a foundation of truth. It is because the enemy of righteousness also works in little steps, so small that they are hard to notice if you are thinking only about yourself and how great you are. Just as truth is given to us line upon line and the light brightens slowly as we obey, even so, as we disobey, our testimony of truth lessens almost imperceptibly, little by little, and darkness descends so slowly that the proud may easily deny that anything is changing.

I have heard the boast of a man who walked away from the Church slowly, at first just ceasing to teach his Sunday School class and then staying away from church and then forgetting tithing now and then. Along the way he would say to me: "I feel just as spiritual as I did before I stopped those things and just as much at peace. Besides, I enjoy Sundays more than I did; it's more a day of rest." Or, "I think I've been blessed temporally as much or more as I was when I was paying tithing." He could not sense the difference, but I could. The light in his eyes and even the shine in his countenance were dimming. He could not tell, since one of the effects of disobeying God seems to be the creation of just enough spiritual anesthetic to block any sensation as the ties to God are being cut. Not only did the testimony of truth slowly erode, but even the memories of what it was like to be in the light began to seem to him like a delusion.

HELPING YOUNG MEN AND YOUNG WOMEN

More than a few of those slides down the path of disobedience come in the years of transition from childhood to maturity. How often have you heard a parent describe a child's tragic journey into years of sin and sorrow by saying, "It began when he was sixteen," or "It began when she was fourteen." And yet in those same years the young man or the young woman who chooses obedience can build a foundation of truth to last in the years ahead, and many do. It is not by accident that seminary across the world is offered to young Latter-day Saints in those years. They are at risk in that time of transition; yet the very source of that risk creates an opportunity for them and for us who serve them.

Agency is the source of that risk. It is so priceless a gift from our Heavenly Father that a war in heaven was fought to defend it. Lucifer sought to take it from us and to take for himself the honor and glory of our Father. The teenager you love may well have been one of the valiant warriors on the side of agency and truth. Satan seems to feel he can win a double victory by drawing teenagers into sin. He can destroy one of his antagonists and in the process try to prove the Father wrong, prove that the risk of agency was too great.

We can help by seeing clearly the opportunity. The teenager who begins to say "It's my life to live, my choices to make" is speaking the truth, a wonderful truth. The choice to do good is the only way to build a life on the foundation of truth and light. Yet these words can strike fear into a parent or a bishop or a Young Women leader who loves the teenager. That outburst of independence usually comes when a rule is announced or something is forbidden. It may come with the mere appearance of authority, of anyone telling them what they must do.

Our opportunity, and theirs, lies in their seeing a simple truth. It is their life to live, and yet they live it with two powerful opposing forces pulling on them. One is from God, who loves and will not compel and who offers eternal life through the plan of salvation. That plan depends on the Atonement made by the Savior, Jesus Christ, and the teenager's choice to follow Him. The other, a terrible power, will use deception, force, and hatred to bring them into bondage and misery. And the teenager is free to choose.

The opportunity is in their seeing that reality, but that is also the problem. It takes the revelation of truth from God for the teenager to see those opposing forces as real. Once seen, the choice will be obvious. But many young people have little experience with persisting in obedience, when the truth must be taken on faith alone until truth is revealed to them. The opportunity lies in their sensing what they once knew, that the power to choose is a gift from God to bring them happiness in this life and in the life to come with Him.

We can help by the way we react to their determination to choose for themselves. They will sense whether we see them as if they could well have been one of the faithful warriors from the premortal existence, committed still to the defense of moral agency and aware of its great value to bring them happiness. If we can see them as faithful warriors from the premortal existence, we may also see their claims of independence as a sign of their potential, a sign that they are testing the power of agency which will bring them happiness. That is hard, because we know the risk should they choose sin. But when fear for them comes, as it does, it helps for us to remember and take comfort that there are opposing pulls. There is an influence of evil in the world, but there is also in the world and across all creation the powerful light of Christ.

A SCRIPTURAL TEST ONE CAN APPLY

Our young people were born with access to the light of Christ. Because of that, they have in them the power to apply for themselves this test given in the book of Moroni, if they believe they can and if they choose to do it:

> Wherefore, all things which are good cometh of God; and that which is evil cometh of the devil; for the devil is an enemy unto God, and fighteth against him continually, and inviteth and enticeth to sin, and to do that which is evil continually.
>
> But behold, that which is of God inviteth and enticeth to do good continually; wherefore, every thing which inviteth and enticeth to do good, and to love God, and to serve him, is inspired of God.

Wherefore, take heed, my beloved brethren, that ye do not judge that which is evil to be of God, or that which is good and of God to be of the devil. (Moroni 7:12–14.)

And then a few verses later:

But whatsoever thing persuadeth men to do evil, and believe not in Christ, and deny him, and serve not God, then ye may know with a perfect knowledge it is of the devil; for after this manner doth the devil work, for he persuadeth no man to do good, no, not one; neither do his angels; neither do they who subject themselves unto him.

And now, my brethren, seeing that ye know the light by which ye may judge, which light is the light of Christ, see that ye do not judge wrongfully; for with that same judgment which ye judge ye shall also be judged. (Moroni 7:17–18.)

The warning not to judge what is of God to be evil nor what is from the devil to be good is a helpful caution to those of us who would help the young learn to choose the right. They will see some choices as good, or at least neutral, which we may see at first as evil. Before we begin to force a choice with what authority we may have, it will be wise to apply the test found in Moroni ourselves. More than once I have been restrained and more than once I have been energized to action by those practical rules. What I at first thought was evil became clear to me as being neutral. And what I had thought was neutral was revealed to me as inviting to do evil. And when the teenager knew I would apply the test myself in humility, it was more likely that they would try the test for themselves.

Our best hope is that they will follow our example of

humbly seeking to know if the choice they are considering will draw them nearer to God or away from Him. If they do what we have done—pray in faith—light and truth will come to them. And if they obey, not only will more truth come but they will have learned how to build their lives on a foundation of truth.

OBEDIENCE

The teenager most likely to have that happy experience will have been given earlier, in childhood, the chance to gain self-discipline enough to persist in obedience, even when at first no good result seems to come. I know now why my mother had me weeding on my knees for what seemed like hours in a wet garden with rows that seemed to stretch to forever, while the weeds broke off in my hand with roots still in the ground. I know now why she smiled so happily when she saw me trying to dig those roots out with my fingers in tearful frustration. She knew something about the teenage years that were coming and what it would take in dogged persistence to build a foundation of light and truth. I don't necessarily recommend weeding or hard labor for little children, but I offer thanks to my mother now, which I was not wise enough to do when I was in the garden.

It would be wrong to suggest that it is easy to help young people obey long enough to qualify for the revelation of truth. Nor can I possibly suggest all that you may be led by the Spirit to do to help them. But I can give this counsel: Above all, you can love them. You can believe and follow the truth in the encouraging view of President Gordon B. Hinckley: "I love the youth of the Church. I have said again and again that

I think we have never had a better generation than this. How grateful I am for your integrity, for your ambition to train your minds and your hands to do good work, for your love for the word of the Lord."

President Hinckley went on to say that he had "tremendous respect for fathers and mothers who are nurturing their children in light and truth, . . . who spare the rod and govern with love, who look upon their little ones as their most valued assets to be protected, trained, and blessed" ("This Is the Work of the Master," *Ensign,* May 1995, 70).

There is a connection between nurturing people in light and truth and the way we teach obedience. Wise mission presidents learn that early. In a mission, obedience is essential for the safety of the missionaries, if for no other reason. There are rules for staying with a companion. There are rules about where a missionary can go. There are rules about driving cars. There are rules about when a missionary should be out of the place he or she lives and when to be back at night and when to go to bed.

The great opportunity in teaching obedience to missionaries is to help them see the connection between the Savior, the companionship of the Spirit, and love. It is to teach them that obedience to the commands of the Father and His Son out of love for Them brings the Spirit. The companionship of the Spirit will bring light and truth, the foundation of successful missionary work and of a happy life. It can be taught in simple matters. Missionaries can put on their seat belts because they remember the safety video from the last zone conference. Or they can do it because they love the mission president and he told them to do it. It is a completely different experience to do it because they think of the Savior's love and that He cares so much for their service and that He loves them so much that He wants them to be safe. The truth is that He needs us. He loves us. When missionaries feel that love of the Savior as they buckle up, they are more than safe in the car. They will be safe against the power of evil in the ministry, and they will be safe against more dangers than traffic accidents. They will have learned obedience to the Lord. They will encounter other rules and there will be other presidents, but the loving Savior will not change, and He will always be there.

Obey Spiritual Promptings

You can test what I am saying. When the Spirit is invited into a meeting, truth is communicated beyond what is said aloud. In your Church meetings, write down impressions or thoughts that you feel came from God. And, remembering what we have said about building a foundation, think carefully about whether the truth you received requires action. It is by obedience to commandments that we qualify for further revelation of truth and light. In a recent meeting you may have committed to act on something you felt was true. Then more truth came to you. That process may slow or stop if, as you go out into daily life, you fail to keep the silent commitments you made with God. God not only loves the obedient, He enlightens them. I fear that more people make promises to God than keep them, so you will please Him when you are the exception and you keep your promise to obey. You should test those impressions of what you should do against a simple standard: Is it what the Master has commanded in the accepted revelations, and is it clearly within my calling in His kingdom?

Keeping some commandments has greater power to build your foundation on truth and light. You could think of those as enabling commandments, because they build your power to keep other commandments. Whatever invites the Holy Ghost to be your companion will bring you greater wisdom and greater ability to obey God. For instance, you are promised that if you always remember the Savior, you will have His Spirit to be with you. You are commanded to pray that you may have the Holy Ghost. You are commanded to pray that you might not be overcome by temptation and so be clean and worthy of the Holy Spirit. You are commanded to study the word of God that you may have His Spirit. I would not set one commandment above another, but I might put some earlier in my efforts if they carry with them the promise of the companionship of the Holy Ghost. The Comforter will lead us to truth and light and will help us obey our Father in Heaven and His Beloved Son. We will come to love Them and those around us as we serve Them, and thus we will keep the great commandments.

Life will have its storms. We can and must have confidence. God our Heavenly Father has given us the right to know the truth. He has shown that the way to receive that truth is simple, so simple that a child can follow it. Once it is followed, more light comes from God to enlighten the understanding of His faithful spirit child. That light will become brighter even as the world darkens. The light that comes to us with truth will be brighter than the darkness that comes from sin and error around us. A foundation built on truth and illuminated by the light of God will free us from the fear that we might be overcome. I promise you that as you obey the commandments, you will know the truth and be strengthened and warmed by light and love, which will come from God.

— 2 —

DO NOT DELAY

All of us have faced deadlines. Fear can grip us when we realize that there may not be enough time left to finish what we promised we would do. The thought comes, "Why didn't I start earlier?"

The Lord knew we would be tempted to procrastinate the most important preparation we could ever make in this life. More than once He warned us about delay. He taught the parable of the ten virgins, five of whom did not fill their lamps for the coming of the bridegroom. He also gave the parable of the servants who were faithless because they believed their Lord would delay His coming. The results of delay were tragic.

For the five unprepared virgins, it was this: "Afterward came also the other virgins, saying, Lord, Lord, open to us. But he answered and said, Verily I say unto you, I know you not" (Matthew 25:11–12).

For the faithless servants who delayed their preparation, it was this: "The lord of that servant shall come in a day when he looketh not for him, and in an hour that he is not

From a talk given at general conference, 2 October 1999.

aware of, and shall cut him asunder, and appoint him his portion with the hypocrites: there shall be weeping and gnashing of teeth" (Matthew 24:50–51).

The temptation to delay repentance comes not only at the end of the world as suggested by those scriptures. That temptation seems to have been nearly constant since the beginning of time and goes on throughout our lives. In youth we may have thought: "There will be time enough to worry about spiritual things just before my mission or before marriage. Spiritual things are for older people." Then, in the early years of marriage, the pressures of life, of jobs, of bills, of finding a moment for rest and recreation seem to crowd us so closely that delay in meeting obligations to God and family again seems reasonable. It is easy to think, "Perhaps there will be more time for that in the middle years." But the compression of time does not ease in the years that follow. There is so much to do, and time seems to shrink. The fifty-fifth birthday and the sixty-fifth and the seventy-fifth don't seem to be a decade apart.

With aging comes physical and emotional challenge. We cannot seem to get as much done in an hour as we did in youth. And it is harder to be patient with others, and they seem more demanding. It is tempting then to excuse ourselves yet again from rising to the standards required by our early covenants, now so long neglected.

Not all of us fall into that trap of inaction. But enough people do that we each have at least one person we love and often more—a child, a parent, a friend—someone for whom we feel responsibility, for whom we ache with concern. They have been taught the gospel. They have made covenants. And yet they go on in disobedience or neglect, despite the emptiness we know that brings them. The choice to repent or to remain a prisoner of sin is their own. Yet knowing something of how the trap of inaction and resistance was built in their minds and hearts may help us hear more easily the answer to our fervent prayer: "Please, Heavenly Father, what can I do to help?"

That temptation to delay comes from our enemy Lucifer. He knows that we can never be truly happy unless we have hope in this life and then realization, in the next, of eternal life. It is the greatest of all the gifts of God. It is to live in families forever with our Heavenly Father and with Jesus Christ and to have eternal increase. Satan wants us to be miserable as he is. And he knows that we can have that true happiness only if we are washed clean through faith in the Lord Jesus Christ, by deep and continuing repentance, and the making and keeping of sacred covenants offered only through God's authorized servants. The scriptures confirm the hazard:

"Wherefore, if ye have sought to do wickedly in the days of your probation, then ye are found unclean before the judgment-seat of God; and no unclean thing can dwell with God; wherefore, ye must be cast off forever" (1 Nephi 10:21).

And so Satan tempts with procrastination throughout our days of probation. Any choice to delay repentance gives him the chance to steal happiness from one of the spirit children of our Heavenly Father.

We have all been tempted with that delay. We know from our own experience that President Spencer W. Kimball was right when he wrote, "One of the most serious human defects in all ages is procrastination," and then he defined it: "an unwillingness to accept personal responsibilities *now*" (*The Teachings of Spencer W. Kimball*, ed. Edward L. Kimball [Salt Lake City: Bookcraft, 1982], 48; emphasis in original). And so Satan works on both our desire to think we have no cause to repent and our desire to push anything unpleasant into the future. He has tempted you and me, and those we love, with thoughts like this: "God is so loving; surely He won't hold me personally responsible for mistakes which are simply the result of being human." And then, if that fails, there is the thought that will almost surely come: "Well, I may be responsible to repent, but this is not a good time to start. If I wait, later will be better."

There are some truths which expose those lies intended to tempt us to procrastinate repentance. Let's start with the deception, which is so attractive, that we have no need to repent.

The truth is that we all need repentance. If we are capable of reason and past the age of eight, we all need the cleansing that comes through applying the full effects of the Atonement of Jesus Christ. When that is clear, we cannot be tricked into delay by the subtle question: "Have I crossed the line of serious sin, or can I put off even thinking about repentance?" The question that really matters is this: "How can I learn to sense even the beginning of sin and so repent early?"

A second truth about our accountability is to know that we are not the helpless victims of our circumstances. The world tries to tell us that the opposite is true: imperfections in our parents or our faulty genetic inheritance are presented to us as absolving us of personal responsibility. But difficult as circumstances may be, they do not relieve us of accountability for our actions or our inactions. Nephi was right. God gives no commandments to the children of men save He prepares a way for them to obey. However difficult our circumstances, we can repent.

Similarly, the world might be willing to excuse our bad behavior because those around us behave badly. It is not true that the behavior of others removes our responsibility for our own. God's standards for our behavior are unchanged whether or not others choose to rise to them.

That becomes especially difficult when others hurt us and we feel justified in our anger. It is a lie that our anger justifies our impulse to hurt or ignore our antagonists. We are to forgive to be forgiven. To wait for them to repent before we forgive and repent is to allow them to choose for us a delay which could cost us happiness here and hereafter.

Finally, we are personally accountable because the Lord has given us ample warning. We receive the Spirit of Christ at birth to tell us right from wrong and to allow us to experience the connection between sin and unhappiness. From the beginning of time He has sent prophets to speak against sin and to invite faith and repentance. He has restored the fulness of the gospel of Jesus Christ through the Prophet Joseph Smith. Gordon B. Hinckley is His living prophet, holding all the keys of the priesthood which allow those who live now to repent and to choose to gain eternal life. We are made accountable this day as the Holy Ghost confirms that these words are true.

Even the acceptance of personal responsibility may not overcome the temptation to believe that now is not the time to repent. "Now" can seem so difficult, and "later" appear so much easier. The truth is that today is always a better day to repent than any tomorrow. First, sin has its debilitating effects on us. The very faith we need to repent is weakened by delay. The choice to continue in sin diminishes our faith and lessens our right to claim the Holy Ghost as our companion and comforter.

And second, even should we be forgiven at some later time, the Lord cannot restore the good effects our repentance today might have had on those we love and are to serve. That is particularly poignant for the parents of young children. In those tender years there are chances for shaping and lifting spirits which may never come again. But even the grandfather who may have missed chances with his own children might, by choosing to repent today, do for grandchildren what he once could have done for their parents.

When responsibility is accepted and the urgency to repent is felt, the question may come, "Where do I start?" Each life is unique. But for all, repentance will surely include passing through the portal of humble prayer. Our Father in Heaven can allow us to feel fully the conviction of our sins. He knows the depths of our remorse. He can then direct what we must do to qualify for forgiveness. For serious sin, we will need to confess to a judge in Israel and accept his guidance. Prayer alone will in that case not be enough. But for all of us, whatever the gravity of our sins, prayer will open the door to repentance and forgiveness. Without earnest prayer, repentance and cleansing are not possible. When the door is opened by prayer, there is possibility for peace.

One of the questions we must ask of our Heavenly

Father in private prayer is this: "What have I done today, or not done, which displeases Thee? If I can only know, I will repent with all my heart without delay." That humble prayer will be answered. And the answers will surely include the assurance that asking today was better than waiting to ask tomorrow.

I testify that the words of a servant of God, spoken long ago, are true:

> And now, my brethren, I would that, after ye have received so many witnesses, seeing that the holy scriptures testify of these things, ye come forth and bring fruit unto repentance.
>
> Yea, I would that ye would come forth and harden not your hearts any longer; for behold, now is the time and the day of your salvation; and therefore, if ye will repent and harden not your hearts, immediately shall the great plan of redemption be brought about unto you.
>
> For behold, this life is the time for men to prepare to meet God; yea, behold the day of this life is the day for men to perform their labors.
>
> And now, as I said unto you before, as ye have had so many witnesses, therefore, I beseech of you that ye do not procrastinate the day of your repentance until the end; for after this day of life, which is given us to prepare for eternity, behold, if we do not improve our time while in this life, then cometh the night of darkness wherein there can be no labor performed.
>
> Ye cannot say, when ye are brought to that awful crisis, that I will repent, that I will return to my God. Nay, ye cannot say this; for that same spirit which doth possess your bodies at the time that ye go out of this life, that same spirit will have power to possess your body in that eternal world. (Alma 34:30–34.)

There is another temptation to be resisted. It is to yield to the despairing thought that it is too hard and too late to repent. I knew a man once who could have thought that and given up. When he was twelve he was ordained a deacon. Some of his friends tempted him to begin to smoke. He began to feel uncomfortable in church. He left his little town, not finishing high school, to begin a life following construction jobs across the United States. He was a heavy-equipment operator. He married. They had children. The marriage ended in a bitter divorce. He lost his children. He lost an eye in an accident. He lived alone in boardinghouses. He lost everything he owned except what he could carry in a trunk.

One night, as he prepared to move yet again, he decided to lighten the load of that trunk. Beneath the junk of years, he found a book. He never knew how it got there. It was the Book of Mormon. He read it through, and the Spirit told him it was true. He knew then that all those years ago he had walked away from the true Church of Jesus Christ and from the happiness which could have been his.

Later, he was my more-than-seventy-year-old district missionary companion. I asked the people we were teaching, as I testified of the power of the Savior's Atonement, to look at him. He had been washed clean and given a new heart, and I knew they would see that in his face. I told the people that what they saw was evidence that the Atonement of Jesus Christ could wash away *all* the corrosive effects of sin.

That was the only time he ever rebuked me. He told me in the darkness outside the trailer where we had been teaching that I should have told the people that while God was able to give him a new heart, He had not been able to give him back his wife and his children and what he might have done for them. But he had not looked back in sorrow and regret for what might have been. He moved forward, lifted by faith, to what yet might be.

One day he told me that in a dream the night before, the sight in his blind eye was restored. He realized that the dream was a glimpse of a future day, walking among loving people in the light of a glorious resurrection. Tears of joy ran down the deeply lined face of that towering, raw-boned man. He spoke to me quietly, with a radiant smile. I don't remember what he said he saw, but I remember that his face shone with happy anticipation as he described the view. With the Lord's help and the miracle of that book in the bottom of a trunk, it had not for him been too late nor the way too hard.

I testify that God the Father lives. I know that. And He loves us. His Only Begotten Son lives. Because He was resurrected, we too will live again. We will see then those we have loved and who have loved us. We can through faith and obedience have family associations forever. Those in our families who love us, on both sides of the veil, would say as we consider whether to humble our hearts and repent, "Please, do not delay." That is the Savior's invitation and His plea.

CHILD OF PROMISE

Since I know something of the anxiety the pressure of time creates in your life, I would like to share what I have learned about how to handle that feeling of hurry. It's important to be sure we agree on the nature of the problem. Time passes at a fixed rate and we can't store it. You can just decide what to do with it—or not to do with it. Even a moment's reflection will help you see that the problem of using your time well is not a problem of the mind but of the heart. It will only yield to a change in the very way we feel about time. The value of time must change for us. And then the way we think about it will change, naturally and wisely.

That change in feeling and in thinking is combined in the words of a prophet of God in this dispensation. It was Brigham Young, and the year was 1877. "The property which we inherit from our Heavenly Father is our time, and the power to choose in the disposition of the same. This is the real capital that is bequeathed unto us by our Heavenly Father; all the rest is what he may be pleased to add unto us" (*Journal of Discourses*, 18:354).

From a talk given at a Brigham Young University fireside, 4 May 1986.

Time is the property which we inherit from God, along with the power to choose what we will do with it. President Young calls the gift of life, which is time and the power to dispose of it, so great an inheritance that we should feel that it is our capital. The early Yankee families in America taught their children and grandchildren some rules about an inheritance. They were always to invest the capital they inherited and to live only on part of the earnings. One rule was "Never spend your capital." The hope was that inherited wealth would be felt a trust so important that no descendant would put pleasure ahead of obligation to those who would follow.

There is more than one way to spend time foolishly, as you know. You may sleep it away or play it away. But the bankruptcy that will cheat all those who follow you comes after the idleness and the thoughtless seeking for thrills.

When you choose to see or hear filth portrayed, for instance, you may at first feel you have just spent some time. But if you persist, you will find that beyond time wasted you have allowed Satan to draw you toward sin and then into it. And then you will have incurred debts that will burden and diminish every minute of existence that follows, unless and until you find the healing balm of the Atonement of Jesus Christ through repentance, which takes pain and time. Oh, what Brigham Young would want for you, and what I pray you may have, is a heart that wants to invest your inheritance—time.

It's worth doing, not only because you have life ahead but because you have eternity ahead as well. Here is one report that suggests your reward for investing your inheritance well here will be to get to do it forever. President Wilford Woodruff gave this report in general conference in 1896:

> Joseph Smith continued visiting myself and others up to a certain time, and then it stopped. The last time I saw him was in heaven. In the night vision I saw him at the door of the temple in heaven. He came to me and spoke to me. He said he could not stop to talk with me because he was in a hurry. The next man I met was Father Smith; he could not talk with me because he was in a hurry. I met half a dozen brethren who had held high positions on earth, and none of them could stop to talk with me because they were in a hurry. I was much astonished. By and by I saw the Prophet again and I got the privilege of asking him a question.
>
> "Now," said I, "I want to know why you are in a hurry. I have been in a hurry all my life; but I expected my hurry would be over when I got into the kingdom of heaven, if I ever did."
>
> Joseph said: "I will tell you, Brother Woodruff. Every dispensation that has had the priesthood on the earth and has gone into the celestial kingdom has had a certain amount of work to do to prepare to go to the earth with the Savior when he goes to reign on the earth. Each dispensation has had ample time to do this work. We have not. We are the last dispensation, and so much work has to be done, and we need to be in a hurry in order to accomplish it."
>
> Of course, that was satisfactory, but it was new doctrine to me. (*Discourses of Wilford Woodruff,* sel. G. Homer Durham [Salt Lake City: Bookcraft, 1946], 288–89.)

Can you see and feel the truth in these familiar words of President Ezra Taft Benson? "You have been born at this time for a sacred and glorious purpose. It is not by chance that you have been reserved to come to earth in this last dispensation of the fulness of times. Your birth at this particular time was foreordained in the eternities.

"You are to be the royal army of the Lord in the last days. You are 'youth of the noble birthright'" ("To the 'Youth of the Noble Birthright,'" *Ensign*, May 1986, 43).

When I heard those words I thought of a boy with a noble birthright, but lacking what many of you have. He was born on November 22. Thirteen days later his father was buried. He was named and blessed by the bishop of his ward, Edwin Woolley. The name he was given by the bishop was Heber Jeddy Ivins Grant. "I was only an instrument in the hands of his dead father . . . in blessing him," Bishop Woolley later remarked. Heber Grant "is entitled to be one of the Apostles, and I know it" (*The Presidents of the Church*, ed. Leonard J. Arrington [Salt Lake City: Deseret Book Co., 1986], 212).

People then and since have called Heber J. Grant a "child of promise." He was. But his departed father didn't make the promises to the child. His Heavenly Father did. Your Heavenly Father did—the same Father who chose you to come into this time and place to hold, honor, and nurture those who hold His power. You have a right to become like your Heavenly Father. You are a royal child of God, a child of promise, chosen from among many to be here and to have your royal inheritance, which includes time in the fulness of times.

One young man changed forever my feelings about the value of that gift and what it means to be a child of promise. Bob Allen was an undergraduate at Stanford University when

I was his bishop. He left his schooling to serve a mission in Japan. He came back to school, took up his studies, and lived in a world of too many demands and too little time.

One day I was sitting at my desk in the graduate school of business at Stanford. I looked up and saw two people. I remember that their faces seemed to shine. Suddenly, Bob Allen stepped between them and, smiling as broadly as they were, said, "These are two new bishops from Japan." They could speak little English, but I could tell they loved Bob Allen and, because of something he must have told them, they loved me. I thought then, as I have many times since, how remarkable it was that he had found time to spend days with those young men from Japan.

I spoke in a sacrament meeting in Tokyo ten years later. The person who had introduced me mentioned that I had been at Stanford. Two young people, a couple, rushed to me after the meeting and said, "Did you know Bob Allen? We love him."

Later I was in Tokyo again. Of all the excellent presentations made to me, one seemed most remarkable. I asked to see the man who had made it. He was introduced and then said, "We have met before, at Stanford University." He was the young man, now older, who had stood with his fellow bishop in my office door. He told me about his life and the life of the other man, now a great leader in Japan. In that moment, I learned again, in my heart as well as my head, what it means to have a royal inheritance of time, and how a child of promise, who believes the promises, can invest it to produce returns for eternity.

Because of that moment I've come to understand something that happened to me in my early teens. I was in a hurry when I felt, not heard, a voice, an impression, which I knew then was from God. It was close to these words: "Someday, when you know who you really are, you will be sorry that you didn't use your time better." I thought then that the impression was odd, since I thought I was using my time pretty well and I thought I knew who I was. Now, years later, I am beginning to know who I am—and who you are—and why we will be so sorry if we do not invest our time well.

You will develop your ability to invest your precious time well by gaining three confidences. First, you must gain confidence that God keeps His promises. Second, you must gain God's confidence that you will always keep the promises, not that you choose to make, but that He asks you to make. And third, you must help others gain confidence that God keeps His promises.

You can gain confidence that God keeps His promises by trying them. That's why I so appreciate those commandments to which God has attached an explicit promise. I see those commandments as school masters. And I try to put them high on my list of things to do, because I know their value for changing my heart and building my power to invest my time.

One of those commandments with promise came to the top of my list awhile back. I was in a sacrament meeting in California. I chose not to spend my time but to invest it. When the young priest blessed the sacrament, I thought of John the Baptist and Joseph Smith. I thought what it means to live in a time when the promise that young man made for me was authorized by God. He said that if I remembered the Savior and kept His commandments, I would always have

His Spirit to be with me. Because I made that promise with faith, and kept it, I had a remarkable week. God kept His promise made by His servant. I hope those two young men in the Palo Alto Ward know that God honored the promise they spoke.

If you are beginning to sense who you are, there are a whole series of things you will be adding at the top of your lists of things to do, if they weren't already there. Reading the Book of Mormon every day, paying tithing, paying a fast offering, and keeping the Sabbath will all be there. And when you carry out those commitments with faith, you will come quickly to know that God keeps His promises.

Now, you might say, "But Brother Eyring, you've just made my problem worse. Now I've added new tasks to my list and I've put them at the top. If my worry before was that I might fail in my work, now I'm even more worried. You know that at least some of the people I'll be competing with will put work first and spiritual things last, or never. Will I always be second-rate in my work if I'm a child of promise?"

You can take comfort. Whenever I've had unusual success in a financial investment, I've started with great partners. Although you are very much the junior partner, you have been invited to invest your time, not alone, but with God. Here is the promise He has made:

"But before ye seek for riches, seek ye for the kingdom of God.

"And after ye have obtained a hope in Christ ye shall obtain riches, if ye seek them; and ye will seek them for the intent to do good—to clothe the naked, and to feed the hungry, and to liberate the captive, and administer relief to the sick and the afflicted" (Jacob 2:18–19).

The promise to you and me in the last days is that after seeking God and serving His children with unwearyingness, we will come to know His will. The promise is not just that I will have the power to do what's on my list of tasks but that I will know what to put there. On those occasions when I have known what should be there, I've found myself glancing at the list as a source of joy, not of anxiety.

Finally, our capacity for investing time well will hinge on our desire to offer others the chance to gain confidence in the promises of God. We've talked about investing time, guided by the promises of God and by our wanting what He wants. What He wants is to bring to pass the immortality and eternal life of man, so much of your time will be invested with the return to come to others. You can take that as a source of great optimism.

First, and perhaps less important, the returns finally do come to you, particularly when you focus on giving instead of getting. You remember the promise in Luke: "Give, and it shall be given unto you; good measure, pressed down, and shaken together, and running over, shall men give into your bosom. For with the same measure that ye mete withal it shall be measured to you again" (Luke 6:38).

But even better you have the promise of Abraham. That guarantees what in financial investments you'd call compounding. An investment compounds when every return goes to work, without your doing anything further to produce more returns. Offering the gospel has the same effect because of the promise made to Abraham and to you.

Abraham was promised both that his seed would hear the gospel and that they would take it to others. Missionaries, mothers, and home teachers invest time that will compound forever.

Now you may object this way: "I go out and make my visits and call on people, but I don't see any results." Another latter-day prophet helped me with that. President David O. McKay said this:

"Man is a spiritual being, a soul, and at some period of his life everyone is possessed with an irresistible desire to know his relationship to the Infinite. . . . There is something within him which urges him to rise above himself, to control his environment, to master the body and all things physical and live in a higher and more beautiful world" (*True to the Faith*, comp. Llewelyn R. McKay [Salt Lake City: Bookcraft, 1966], 244).

Even people who seem careless and uninterested in spiritual things will at some time reach out to know who they are and who God is and whether they are a child of God and whether there really are promises. You won't know when, but it will come.

Some of you have invested months and years trying to offer people you love the gospel of Jesus Christ—to people who have not yet accepted it. Take heart. Alma the Younger, when he came to the point of extremity, remembered the words of his father and it saved his eternal life. God may yet bless you with that greatest of all returns for the investment of your time, that the words of truth you spoke will be remembered in that moment of spiritual yearning by the person you loved enough to offer the most precious thing you ever received.

We have talked about investing your inheritance—the time that God has given you—and the power you have to dispose of it wisely. Tonight and tomorrow and the next day you and I will ask God what to do with our time. I promise you that he will answer those prayers, because he is in need of servants to reach out to his children. Don't be surprised if he asks you to reach out to them with kindness and with the gospel of Jesus Christ. You can be confident that the promises he has made will be fulfilled. He will, through you, touch the hearts of others, if not always on the timetable you would choose. And they will then, in turn, be touched and reach out to others, multiplying the effects of your investment of time and effort and faith.

Now, I haven't solved the problem of your busy schedules. You will still feel that you are in a hurry, and you will still find yourself not reaching the end of every list. In fact, you may find your list changing and even growing larger. But you can have peace and confidence in your choices. I pray that you will feel that peace and that you will feel gratitude for having been blessed with the restored gospel of Jesus Christ, with living prophets, and with the sure promise of the Atonement of the Lord Jesus Christ. And I pray that you will have confidence in God's promises, gain His confidence, and offer to others the promises you have as a child of promise.

— 4 —

MAKING COVENANTS
WITH GOD

Ll of us can remember times in our lives when we felt a pull to be better than we were, to rise higher. The feeling may have come at about the same time we had the thought, "There must be something better in life than this." Sadly, there have also been times when we felt like giving up. And then the thought was something like, "Maybe this feeling of being miserable is what life is really like. Maybe I need to learn to live with it. It looks as if that's how everyone else feels. Those movies about feeling good and those people who look happy have bought into an illusion." I remember there was even a T-shirt made with a slogan on the front saying, "Life is hard and then it's over." And the look on the man's face wearing it made it seem that he was living proof.

But everyone that I have come to know well, even the most discouraged and the most miserable, will tell you that some time in their lives, maybe just once that they can remember, they felt that upward pull, that thought that there just had to be something better and higher.

From a talk given at a Brigham Young University fireside, 8 September 1996.

The feeling that you are meant to be better, perhaps in a way you haven't yet discovered, comes from our Heavenly Father. The opposing thought, that the upward pull is an illusion, comes from the adversary, who wants us all to be miserable, as he is.

Heavenly Father does more than allow you to feel that upward pull. He has provided a way to rise higher, almost beyond our limits of imagination, not by our own powers alone, which would not be nearly enough, but through the power of the atonement of His Son, Jesus Christ. His prophets have described that gift to us in many ways, but this passage both teaches the idea and gives us that feeling again that there is a way to rise above where we are:

> I say unto you, if ye have come to a knowledge of the goodness of God, and his matchless power, and his wisdom, and his patience, and his long-suffering towards the children of men; and also, the atonement which has been prepared from the foundation of the world, that thereby salvation might come to him that should put his trust in the Lord, and should be diligent in keeping his commandments, and continue in the faith even unto the end of his life, I mean the life of the mortal body—
>
> I say, that this is the man who receiveth salvation, through the atonement which was prepared from the foundation of the world for all mankind, which ever were since the fall of Adam, or who are, or who ever shall be, even unto the end of the world. (Mosiah 4:6–7.)

This scripture beautifully describes why you are justified in your hope of changing, of being lifted to a higher plane of living. In another place, in the Doctrine and Covenants, the Lord describes how we can choose to receive His gift and be lifted toward Him and our Father in Heaven. Here are the words that describe that process: "These are they who are just men made perfect through Jesus the mediator of the new covenant, who wrought out this perfect atonement through the shedding of his own blood" (D&C 76:69).

Our Heavenly Father not only provided a savior and a gospel of Jesus Christ that teaches us the purpose of life and gives us commandments, but He provided covenants we could make with Him. And with those covenants He provided ordinances where He could signify what He promised or covenanted to do and we could signify what we promised or covenanted to do. All of those covenants, taken together, are a "new and everlasting covenant" (D&C 132:6).

Our Heavenly Father has at different periods in the history of this earth adjusted what He has asked of His children because of choices they made, but the new and everlasting covenant has endured and will endure. Here it is described by the Lord as the gospel of Jesus Christ was being restored for the last time: "Behold, I say unto you that all old covenants have I caused to be done away in this thing; and this is a new and an everlasting covenant, even that which was from the beginning" (D&C 22:1).

Heavenly Father has always helped His children by offering them covenants and empowering His servants to offer ordinances. President Marion G. Romney named some of those covenants as he described the kindness of our Father in Heaven and of the Savior:

"Traditionally, God's people have been known as a covenant people. The gospel itself is the new and everlasting covenant. The posterity of Abraham through Isaac and Jacob is the covenant race. We come into the Church by covenant, which we enter into when we go into the waters of baptism. The new and everlasting covenant of celestial marriage is the gate to exaltation in the celestial kingdom. Men receive the Melchizedek Priesthood by an oath and covenant" (in Conference Report, April 1962, 17).

My message to you in these pages is one of gratitude to our Heavenly Father and His Son, Jesus Christ, for offering to make those covenants with us, and it is one of joy that those covenants are what you have always wanted, are what you yearned for when you felt those stirrings for a better life.

My concern is that if we look only at the promises we make, the magnitude of them could overwhelm and perhaps even discourage. Sadly, many of us have seen that happen. We have taught the gospel to someone who understood and believed it but shrank back at the thought of taking on the obligations that come with the ordinance and the covenants of baptism. It takes issuing the baptismal challenge to just a few contacts to have the experience of seeing concern in the eyes of even a believing person. Perhaps that is why Alma the Elder issued his invitation to accept the obligations of the baptismal covenant in the beautiful way that he did. It is recorded this way:

> And it came to pass that he said unto them: Behold, here are the waters of Mormon (for thus were they called) and now, as ye are desirous to come into the fold of God, and to be called his people, and are willing to bear one another's burdens, that they may be light;
> Yea, and are willing to mourn with those that mourn; yea, and comfort those that stand in need of comfort, and to stand as witnesses of God at all times and in all things,

and in all places that ye may be in, even until death, that ye may be redeemed of God, and be numbered with those of the first resurrection, that ye may have eternal life—

Now I say unto you, if this be the desire of your hearts, what have you against being baptized in the name of the Lord, as a witness before him that ye have entered into a covenant with him, that ye will serve him and keep his commandments, that he may pour out his Spirit more abundantly upon you? (Mosiah 18:8–10.)

Alma knew what it takes not only to be willing but also to love to make covenants with God. He didn't minimize the obligations: a lifetime of reaching out to every soul whom God may call us to serve, both with comfort and with fearless declaration of the truthfulness of the gospel of Jesus Christ as God has revealed it to His authorized servants. The person contemplating such a life can sense what it will take in effort and in courage. Alma knew they would see that, and so he also told them what we need to hear, too. Notice at the end, in only a few words, he told them what God would covenant to do as they kept their part of the covenant: "That he may pour out his Spirit more abundantly upon you."

The people he was inviting to the covenant of baptism had already tasted the sweet promptings of the Holy Ghost. Alma gave a promise that is sure: If they would make and keep the covenant in the waters of baptism, they would then be able to receive the ordinance of the laying on of hands for the gift of the Holy Ghost. And then they would not only have an increase in the power and frequency of those sweet promptings of the Comforter, but they could have the promise fulfilled to them of the Holy Ghost as a companion. With every covenant there are great and sure promises from our

Heavenly Father. Alma must have known that those people could anticipate, and so would want, a life where the Holy Ghost could be a companion.

But he taught more than that. Listen to the words with which he began: "As ye are desirous to come into the fold of God, and to be called his people." Alma knew the covenant was not like a business deal—"you do this for God, and God will do this for you"—but it was an opportunity for them to become His, to become God's people. Every covenant with God is an opportunity to draw closer to Him. To anyone who reflects for a moment on what they have already felt of the love of God, to have that bond made stronger and that relationship closer is an irresistible offer. Alma knew the people he taught had felt and recognized the love of God. We may not recognize it, but when our faith lets us see the evidence of God's love in His blessings, we will be as eager to make a covenant to draw closer to Him as were the people at the waters of Mormon.

That upward pull we have felt is far more than a desire for self-improvement. It is a longing for home, to be again with our Heavenly Father, whom we have loved and who loves us, and to be able to live again with Him, feeling the love we felt there and that we can taste here, if we will. And all of us sense the mighty change that must come in us for us to be able to dwell with Him again.

We can find that same pattern of describing obligations, promises, and the assurance of growing closer to God in the way the Lord offers us other covenants. The Melchizedek Priesthood is offered with an oath and covenant. You can hear words describing both promised blessings and the assurance of drawing closer to God to become more like Him, as well as the obligations we assume:

> For whoso is faithful unto the obtaining these two priesthoods of which I have spoken, and the magnifying their calling, are sanctified by the Spirit unto the renewing of their bodies.
>
> They become the sons of Moses and of Aaron and the seed of Abraham, and the church and kingdom, and the elect of God.
>
> And also all they who receive this priesthood receive me, saith the Lord;
>
> For he that receiveth my servants receiveth me;
>
> And he that receiveth me receiveth my Father;
>
> And he that receiveth my Father receiveth my Father's kingdom; therefore all that my Father hath shall be given unto him.
>
> And this is according to the oath and covenant which belongeth to the priesthood.
>
> Therefore, all those who receive the priesthood, receive this oath and covenant of my Father, which he cannot break, neither can it be moved.
>
> But whoso breaketh this covenant after he hath received it, and altogether turneth therefrom, shall not have forgiveness of sins in this world nor in the world to come.
>
> And wo unto all those who come not unto this priesthood which ye have received, which I now confirm upon you who are present this day, by mine own voice out of the heavens; and even I have given the heavenly hosts and mine angels charge concerning you. (D&C 84:33–42.)

The magnitude of the promises available through that covenant make the heart beat a little faster. Here are just a few.

When we honor the priesthood, we have heavenly hosts and angels who are watching over us. Some of us know how literally that is true. There are some returned missionaries who know that they have walked down some streets and been in some places and faced some anger and opposition where they have felt protection and have been watched over by more than human power. Some of us have an absolute assurance that those whom we have known who held the priesthood who are now part of that heavenly host are deeply aware of what we are doing and sometimes deeply concerned for the quality of our service.

Also, the promise is there that those who receive the servants of God, honoring that priesthood, will have this blessing:

"For he that receiveth my servants receiveth me;

"And he that receiveth me receiveth my Father;

"And he that receiveth my Father receiveth my Father's kingdom; therefore all that my Father hath shall be given unto him" (D&C 84:36–38).

There, again, is the promise that is in all the covenants that God offers to us to make with Him: Keeping them will draw us up, closer to Him. And even a small recognition of His love makes us want to make covenants with Him and to keep them. That love more than wipes out the fear that the magnitude of our promises and the severity of the penalties for failure could create in us.

The covenant God offers us in marriage contains the crowning promise, the one that most touches our hearts. To be sealed in the temple of God by the sealing power that God has restored to the earth allows God to promise us that we may have all that He has, may live the life that He lives, and may be with Him, the Savior, and our faithful family members forever in perfect love and harmony. Our promise is complete, too. We promise to give Him all that we have and are and all that we may ever have and ever achieve. So the promise is that we may have all He has by giving all we have. The almost unimaginable imbalance of that exchange, all we have for all He has, is a measure of His love for us. That ought to increase that upward tug we've felt in the way a prophet long ago described feeling in his heart:

"Yea, methought I saw, even as our father Lehi saw, God sitting upon his throne, surrounded with numberless concourses of angels, in the attitude of singing and praising their God; yea, and my soul did long to be there" (Alma 36:22).

All of us are blessed by these covenants, whatever our circumstances. There were in the central part of Africa people who could not accept the baptismal covenant because those authorized to administer that ordinance were not yet among them. But they studied the scriptures of the Restoration as well as the Bible, learned all they could, lived what they understood, and waited. The opportunity to be baptized finally came. They had prepared. Each time I go to the temple to perform an ordinance by proxy for a dead ancestor, I pray that somehow the faithful elders in the spirit world have found them, that they have anticipated this day, and that in their hearts they have been prepared to make and keep the covenants.

The same is true for the oath and covenant of the priesthood and the covenant of marriage in the temple. There might be some young woman reading this with the thought,

"What has that got to do with me?" But then you may have friends whose lives could be changed forever by how you feel about the oath and covenant of the priesthood and the covenant of marriage in the house of the Lord. You may have more influence than you can imagine on a young man's keeping the oath and covenant of the priesthood and on whether he will know the joy of making covenants in the temple. If you love those covenants, he is more likely to love and honor them.

All of us need to increase our desire to make covenants with God. A place to begin is to recognize some things that have already happened to each of us. That stirring we have felt to be better, the thought that there must be some higher life and better place, is a gift of faith in covenants with God. We could ask God in prayer to confirm that this is true and that the feeling came from Him.

Another recognition of what is past that will increase our desire to keep covenants is to see more clearly the evidence of God's love for us in what He has done already.

That can be hard. The world tries to tell us that whatever good happens is from our own efforts. And then, in a quick reversal of logic—from the claim that there is no God to the suggestion that He is heartless—the world will say to us, "How can you believe in a God of justice and mercy when such bad things happen to you and to others?" On top of the world trying to get us to believe God couldn't be the author of our blessings, our natural selfishness can distract us from recognizing and feeling His love. We can focus so much on what we have asked for, which He either hasn't given yet or may never give because it is not good for us, that we ignore the blessings He has already showered upon us. If we would like to increase our desire to make covenants with God by sensing more clearly His love for us, we ought to read frequently some words of King Benjamin. You will remember them, since they are familiar, but you might read them this time not for the rebuke that is there but for the invitation to see ourselves as children favored by a loving Father:

> I say unto you, my brethren, that if you should render all the thanks and praise which your whole soul has power to possess, to that God who has created you, and has kept and preserved you, and has caused that ye should rejoice, and has granted that ye should live in peace one with another—
>
> I say unto you that if ye should serve him who has created you from the beginning, and is preserving you from day to day, by lending you breath, that ye may live and move and do according to your own will, and even supporting you from one moment to another—I say, if ye should serve him with all your whole souls yet ye would be unprofitable servants.
>
> And behold, all that he requires of you is to keep his commandments; and he has promised you that if ye would keep his commandments ye should prosper in the land; and he never doth vary from that which he hath said; therefore, if ye do keep his commandments he doth bless you and prosper you.
>
> And now, in the first place, he hath created you, and granted unto you your lives, for which ye are indebted unto him.
>
> And secondly, he doth require that ye should do as he hath commanded you; for which if ye do, he doth immediately bless you; and therefore he hath paid you. And ye

are still indebted unto him, and are, and will be, forever and ever; therefore, of what have ye to boast?

And now I ask, can ye say aught of yourselves? I answer you, Nay. Ye cannot say that ye are even as much as the dust of the earth; yet ye were created of the dust of the earth; but behold, it belongeth to him who created you.

And I, even I, whom ye call your king, am no better than ye yourselves are; for I am also of the dust. And ye behold that I am old, and am about to yield up this mortal frame to its mother earth. (Mosiah 2:20–26.)

You and I could choose to see Heavenly Father and our lives that way. Even as his mortal body was failing, King Benjamin saw that every covenant he had kept had brought the promised blessings. But on top of that he had received the blessings God pours out on all His children, without regard to their station or even their gratitude. If we could just train ourselves to see as King Benjamin saw, it wouldn't be hard to keep what the Savior described once as the first commandment: "And thou shalt love the Lord thy God with all thy heart, and with all thy soul, and with all thy mind, and with all thy strength: this is the first commandment" (Mark 12:30).

We can start down the King Benjamin road today by counting our blessings. We could try naming them one by one in prayer, perhaps pausing a moment after each one to let the feelings of gratitude grow. We may be surprised not only by what the Lord has done but by how long we have been kneeling there as the blessings we have not noticed or have forgotten come flooding into our minds. The covenant promise the Lord made that His disciples could remember His words extends to remembering and recognizing His blessings. I know because I have tried it. Here is the promise as recorded in John: "But the Comforter, which is the Holy Ghost, whom the Father will send in my name, he shall teach you all things, and bring all things to your remembrance, whatsoever I have said unto you" (John 14:26).

The feeling of gratitude and love which will come from that prayer will move us toward wanting to make and keep covenants with God. Those who are not yet members of the Church will be drawn to pray to ask whether the power to baptize was restored through John the Baptist conferring the Aaronic Priesthood upon Joseph Smith and Oliver Cowdery and whether the power to confer the gift of the Holy Ghost was returned to the earth by Peter, James, and John. Those of us who have been baptized will review our lives to see what we have done or not done that determines whether the Lord can keep His promise to let the Spirit always be with us. Because we are human still, that reflection usually leads to a desire to repent of things both done and not done.

If we repeat the process often enough and with enough intent, we will feel some desires to honor the oath and covenant of the priesthood. The oath and covenant has blessings in it for all of us, young and old, whatever our situations. You remember the promise:

"For he that receiveth my servants receiveth me;

"And he that receiveth me receiveth my Father;

"And he that receiveth my Father receiveth my Father's kingdom; therefore all that my Father hath shall be given unto him" (D&C 84:36–38).

There is a blessing for us in such a small act as inviting a home teacher to give a blessing or asking a bishop if there is any way we could help him in his service. There is a blessing in the way we speak of the prophet of God and in whether we listen when he speaks. We can receive the Lord's servants during general conference simply by yearning to hear their words or by reading them and pondering when we can. When we receive the Lord's servants, we receive Him. In that we are all blessed, or we can be, by the promises in the oath and covenant of the priesthood.

Within the family there may be for us greater opportunities to welcome the powers promised through the priesthood and thus to welcome the Lord. Every person in a family has an effect on the power of the priesthood exercised there. For a solitary member it may be to ask for a home teacher to give a priesthood blessing. For the child of a father growing indifferent to his priesthood covenants it may be the quiet request, "Dad, I'd like you to be with me when I go to the temple," or "Dad, it would mean so much to me if you could set me apart." More than one man has started upward again, never to turn back, after hearing and feeling such a plea from his child.

The covenant of a temple marriage may seem distant, either because it appears unattainable or because the cares of a busy life have eroded the meaning it had when the covenants were made. But every child of God is promised every blessing if he or she is faithful. And where those covenants have been made, the blessings are still available. In just the last few days I heard a young girl report a night of babysitting. That doesn't sound very celestial, and it had its challenges for her. But the reports of little kindnesses shown, of patience, of long-suffering, made me think of a passage of scripture that may not have occurred to her that night. It goes this way:

"No power or influence can or ought to be maintained by virtue of the priesthood, only by persuasion, by long-suffering, by gentleness and meekness, and by love unfeigned" (D&C 121:41).

This young girl may not have been thinking of marriage and of the home she may someday have, of children, and of a priesthood holder in it as her companion. But she was choosing that night to live in such a way that if someday God gave her such blessings, those children and that husband would experience and expect, simply by her example, the kind of care that is given by the true servants of God. And if she were so blessed, her husband would be drawn upward in his priesthood service just by what that little girl, grown older, would bring to that home and family.

We can do the things now that will lead us to love, make, and keep covenants. And we can without invading their agency invite others by example to love and want to make and keep covenants. Because of what we do, they can look forward to the peace and the hope that can come from keeping the baptismal covenant, from receiving those who honor the oath and covenant of the priesthood, and from associating in a home where people are living so that they might be sealed to live forever in the presence of our Heavenly Father and His Son, Jesus Christ.

— 5 —

PRAYER

The world seems to be in commotion. There are wars and rumors of wars. The economies of whole continents are faltering. Crops are failing from lack of rain in places all over the earth. And the people in peril have flooded heaven with prayers. In public and in private, they are petitioning God for help, for comfort, and for direction.

You have probably noticed, as I have in recent days, that prayers have not only become more numerous but more heartfelt. I often am seated on the stand in a meeting near the person who has been asked to pray. I have listened recently with wonder. The words spoken are clearly inspired by God, both eloquent and wise. And the tone is that of a loving child seeking help, not as we might from an earthly parent but from an all-powerful Heavenly Father who knows our needs before we ask.

Such a turning to fervent prayer when the world seems out of joint is as old as mankind. In times of tragedy and danger, people turn to God in prayer. Even the ancient King

From a talk given at general conference, 6 October 2001.

David would recognize what is happening. You remember his words from the book of Psalms:

"The Lord also will be a refuge for the oppressed, a refuge in times of trouble.

"And they that know thy name will put their trust in thee: for thou, Lord, hast not forsaken them that seek thee" (Psalm 9:9–10).

The great increase in heartfelt prayer, and the public acceptance of it, has been remarkable to me and to others. More than once in recent days, someone has said to me with great intensity and with a sound of worry in the voice, "I hope that the change lasts."

That worry is justified. Our own personal experience and God's record of His dealing with His children teaches us that. Dependence on God can fade quickly when prayers are answered. And when the trouble lessens, so do the prayers. The Book of Mormon repeats that sad story over and over again.

From the book of Helaman, "O, how could you have forgotten your God in the very day that he has delivered you?" (Helaman 7:20). And later from the same book, after God had answered prayers with gracious kindness, the awful pattern is described again:

> And thus we can behold how false, and also the unsteadiness of the hearts of the children of men; yea, we can see that the Lord in his great infinite goodness doth bless and prosper those who put their trust in him.
>
> Yea, and we may see at the very time when he doth prosper his people, yea, in the increase of their fields, their flocks and their herds, and in gold, and in silver, and in all manner of precious things of every kind and

art; sparing their lives, and delivering them out of the hands of their enemies; softening the hearts of their enemies that they should not declare wars against them; yea, and in fine, doing all things for the welfare and happiness of his people; yea, then is the time that they do harden their hearts, and do forget the Lord their God, and do trample under their feet the Holy One—yea, and this because of their ease, and their exceedingly great prosperity.

And thus we see that except the Lord doth chasten his people with many afflictions, yea, except he doth visit them with death and with terror, and with famine and with all manner of pestilence, they will not remember him. (Helaman 12:1–3.)

And now, from the next words of that same scripture, we learn why it is we forget so easily the source of our blessings and cease to feel our need to pray with faith:

O how foolish, and how vain, and how evil, and how devilish, and how quick to do iniquity, and how slow to do good, are the children of men; yea, how quick to hearken unto the words of the evil one, and to set their hearts upon the vain things of the world!

Yea, how quick to be lifted up in pride; yea, how quick to boast, and do all manner of that which is iniquity; and how slow are they to remember the Lord their God, and to give ear unto his counsels, yea, how slow to walk in wisdom's paths!

Behold, they do not desire that the Lord their God, who hath created them, should rule and reign over them; notwithstanding his great goodness and his mercy towards them, they do set at naught his counsels, and they will not that he should be their guide. (Helaman 12:4–6.)

From those three short verses of scripture, we see three causes for the sad drift away from humble prayer. First, while God implores us to pray, the enemy of our souls belittles and then derides it. The warning from 2 Nephi is true: "And now, my beloved brethren, I perceive that ye ponder still in your hearts; and it grieveth me that I must speak concerning this thing. For if ye would hearken unto the Spirit which teacheth a man to pray ye would know that ye must pray; for the evil spirit teacheth not a man to pray, but teacheth him that he must not pray" (2 Nephi 32:8).

Second, God is forgotten out of vanity. A little prosperity and peace, or even a turn slightly for the better, can bring us feelings of self-sufficiency. We can feel quickly that we are in control of our lives, that the change for the better is our own doing, not that of a God who communicates to us through the still, small voice of the Spirit. Pride creates a noise within us which makes the quiet voice of the Spirit hard to hear. And soon, in our vanity, we no longer even listen for it. We can come quickly to think we don't need it.

The third cause is rooted deeply within us. We are spirit children of a loving Heavenly Father who placed us in mortality to see if we would choose—freely choose—to keep His commandments and come unto His Beloved Son. They do not compel us. They cannot, for that would interfere with the plan of happiness. And so there is in us a God-given desire to be responsible for our own choices.

That desire to make our own choices is part of the upward pull toward eternal life. But it can, if we see life only through our mortal eyes, make dependence on God difficult or even impossible when we feel such a powerful desire to be independent. This true doctrine can sound hard:

"For the natural man is an enemy to God, and has been from the fall of Adam, and will be, forever and ever, unless he yields to the enticings of the Holy Spirit, and putteth off the natural man and becometh a saint through the atonement of Christ the Lord, and becometh as a child, submissive, meek, humble, patient, full of love, willing to submit to all things which the Lord seeth fit to inflict upon him, even as a child doth submit to his father" (Mosiah 3:19).

Those who submit like a child do it because they know that the Father wants only the happiness of His children and that only He knows the way. That is the testimony we must have to keep praying like a submissive child, in the good times as well as the times of trouble.

With that faith, we will be able to pray for what we want and appreciate whatever we get. Only with that faith will we pray with the diligence God requires. When God has commanded us to pray, He has used words like "pray unceasingly" and "pray always" and "mighty prayer."

Those commands do not require using many words. In fact, the Savior has told us that we need not multiply words when we pray. The diligence in prayer which God requires does not take flowery speech or long hours of solitude. That is taught clearly in Alma in the Book of Mormon: "Yea, and when you do not cry unto the Lord, let your hearts be full, drawn out in prayer unto him continually for your welfare, and also for the welfare of those who are around you" (Alma 34:27).

Our hearts can be drawn out to God only when they are

filled with love for Him and trust in His goodness. Joseph Smith, even as a boy, gave us an example of how we can come to pray from a heart filled with the love of God and then pray unceasingly through a life filled with trials and blessings.

Joseph started for the grove to pray with faith that a loving God would answer his prayer and relieve his confusion. He gained that assurance reading the word of God and receiving a witness that it was true. He said that he read in James, "Let him ask of God, that giveth to all men liberally, and upbraideth not; and it shall be given him" (James 1:5; Joseph Smith–History 1:11). His faith to ask of God in prayer came after pondering a scripture which assured him of God's loving nature. He prayed, as we must, with faith in a loving God.

He prayed with the intent not only to listen but to obey. He did not ask only to *know* the truth. He was committed to *act* upon whatever God would communicate to him. His written account makes clear that he prayed with real intent, determined to comply with whatever answer he received. He wrote:

> Never did any passage of scripture come with more power to the heart of man than this did at this time to mine. It seemed to enter with great force into every feeling of my heart. I reflected on it again and again, knowing that if any person needed wisdom from God, I did; for how to act I did not know, and unless I could get more wisdom than I then had, I would never know; for the teachers of religion of the different sects understood the same passages of scripture so differently as to destroy all confidence in settling the question by an appeal to the Bible. (Joseph Smith–History 1:12.)

The Father and His Beloved Son appeared to Joseph in answer to his prayer. And he was told how to act, as he had desired. He obeyed like a child. He was told to join none of the churches. He did as he was told. And because of his faithfulness, in the days and months and years ahead his prayers were answered with a flood of light and truth. The fulness of the gospel of Jesus Christ and the keys of the kingdom of God were restored to the earth. His humble dependence on God led to the Restoration of the gospel, with authority and sacred ordinances. Because of that Restoration, we have the chance to choose the most priceless independence—to be free of the bondage of sin through the cleansing power of the Atonement of Jesus Christ.

Joseph Smith's mission was unique, yet his humble prayer can be a helpful model for us. He began, as we must, with faith in a loving God who can and wants to communicate with us and help us. That faith was rooted in impressions that came to him as he pondered the words of God's servants in the scriptures. We can and must go often and carefully to the word of God. If we become casual in our study of the scriptures, we will become casual in our prayers.

We may not cease to pray, but our prayers will become more repetitive, more mechanical, lacking real intent. Our hearts cannot be drawn out to a God we do not know, and the scriptures and the words of living prophets help us know Him. As we know Him better, we love Him more.

We must also serve Him to love Him. Joseph Smith did that, finally surrendering life itself in His service. Joseph prayed with the intent to obey. That obedience always includes service to others. Service in God's work allows us to feel a part of what He feels and come to know Him.

"For how knoweth a man the master whom he has not served, and who is a stranger unto him, and is far from the thoughts and intents of his heart?" (Mosiah 5:13). As our love for Him increases, so will our desire to approach the Father in prayer.

The words and the music of our Church meetings will lead you to do what will strengthen you against the danger of a drift away from heartfelt prayer. From what you hear you will feel promptings to go to the scriptures. Follow the promptings. You will be reminded in Church meetings of service you committed to give when you entered the waters of baptism. Choose to obey.

If you ponder the scriptures and begin to do what you covenanted with God to do, I can promise you that you will feel more love for God and more of His love for you. And with that, your prayers will come from the heart, full of thanks and of pleading. You will feel a greater dependence on God. You will find the courage and the determination to act in His service, without fear and with peace in your heart. You will pray always. And you will not forget Him, no matter what the future brings.

— 6 —

ALWAYS

Years ago I served as the bishop of a ward composed of young people. Time has wiped away much of what I learned then of their sorrows and mistakes, but I can still see in my mind most of their faces. I meet some of them as I travel about the world. Their faces and their physiques have been changed enough by time that I sometimes stumble trying to remember names. Others I have followed more closely, with a chance to know what life has offered them. When I learn of their lives, I am amazed at the variety of their experiences. Each life seems unique. About all they have in common, as nearly as I can tell, is that they have been surprised by the pattern of the tests of their faith. The surprises have come because they could not know when the tests would occur, what they would be, or how long they would last.

For some members of that ward, the tests ended early. I was reminded of one young man the other day. For me his face will always be young and bright with hope. He left our ward for a mission in Japan. Decades later I mentioned his

From a talk given at a Church Educational System fireside at Brigham Young University, 3 January 1999.

name in a talk I gave to a group of Latter-day Saints in Tokyo. After the meeting a number of members came to me, their faces shining with the brightness that I remember in his face when he returned from his mission. They told me he was "their" missionary. If I understood their English, they said he was the greatest missionary they had ever known.

I was released as the bishop when our family was asked to move to another state. I kept track of that missionary enough to know that he had graduated from college, applied to medical school, and been accepted. I did not know his plans for the summer before he began medical school, but I am sure he looked forward with great anticipation to the years ahead.

A phone rang where we then lived, and I learned that he had been killed. He and friends had gone to climb a peak in the Wind River Range in the western United States. I was invited to speak at his funeral. I asked some of the young men who had been climbing with him, friends from our old ward family, to join me at the meetinghouse where the service would begin. We went to a room to be alone. After we had renewed our acquaintance, I asked if they would tell me something about our friend's life. I think they knew why.

I wished to speak in the funeral about him and his life. They knew how much I had admired him. They also knew I had not seen him or spoken with him for a few years. They knew that I wanted to praise him but that the praise had to be true.

They told me this story: They had camped out for the night in preparation for the ascent to the peak. As they climbed high on the face of the mountain, a storm came upon them. They could not see their way because of the clouds and the storm. Our friend had volunteered to go alone to find the path. He didn't come back. They found later that he had fallen to his death, trying to save his friends.

Then, without my prompting, they told me of more than his courage. They told me of where he had been on the trail of faith. They said that the night before the climb, while others had talked quietly and prepared for sleep, he had been studying his scriptures and his missionary lessons in Japanese.

I suppose that in the time after his mission he had the trials and the temptations that are common to returned missionaries. The fact that he had applied to medical school makes it clear to me that he thought the tests of life stretched far ahead of him. Yet when life ended, he was ready.

I think of this young man often. A stake president who was his friend in youth met me not long ago in Virginia. I heard the same sound of love and awe in his voice that I heard from the members in Tokyo and from his fellow mountain climbers.

When such a life touches ours, we are never the same again. We want somehow to be as constant in our faith as he was. We want to know the way to endure whatever surprises life may give us, always ready with the power to pass the tests that come, always faithful, whatever the tests, to the end—whenever that may be.

THE WORD *ALWAYS*

The Savior has used the word *always* in two settings that must have caused you to wonder. First, in every sacrament meeting the word *always* is used in a covenant, a sacred promise with God that you are making. This is what you hear, read by authorized servants of God: "That they are willing to take upon them the name of thy Son, and *always* remember him and keep his commandments which he has given them; that they may *always* have his Spirit to be with them. Amen" (D&C 20:77; emphasis added).

Another setting in which the word *always* is used is in a commandment. The Lord repeats the command often, with only slight variations. Here is one of them: "Behold, verily, verily, I say unto you, ye must watch and pray *always* lest ye enter into temptation; for Satan desireth to have you, that he may sift you as wheat" (3 Nephi 18:18; emphasis added).

You promise to "always remember him." And He warns you to "pray always." You may have wondered, as have I, why He used the word *always*, given the nature of mortality as it weighs upon us. You know from experience how hard it is to think of anything consciously all the time. Even in service to God, you will not be consciously praying always. So why does the Master exhort us to "pray always"?

I am not wise enough to know all of His purposes in giving us a covenant to always remember Him and in warning us to pray always lest we be overcome. But I know one. It is because He knows perfectly the powerful forces that influence us and also what it means to be human.

OPPOSING FORCES

You and I can see evidence of the acceleration in the two great opposing forces around us. One is the force of righteousness. For instance, temples of God are being built across the earth at a rate that just a few years ago would have been unthinkable. Missionaries are being called in numbers and to new places which change so rapidly that I have learned not to try to give the numbers or the places because my knowledge will have fallen behind the reality. Leaders of nations and opinion makers in the media seem to see that which was prophesied by the Lord to the Prophet Joseph Smith in the infant days of the Church: "And also those to whom these commandments were given, might have power to lay the foundation of this church, and to bring it forth out of obscurity and out of darkness, the only true and living church upon the face of the whole earth, with which I, the Lord, am well pleased, speaking unto the church collectively and not individually" (D&C 1:30).

Even the world can see the emergence of a power beyond what might have been reasonably predicted. Yet few seem to recognize that the power stems not from organization or programs or wealth. Rather, it comes from individual hearts changed by faith to keep the commandments of the gospel of Jesus Christ.

As has always been true, there is an opposing power. It is the power of sin, and it is visibly accelerating. I will not try to bring examples to your minds. The media and what you see in the lives of those around you present you with tragedy enough. And even in your experience, you surely must sense the ominous increase of toleration and even encouragement of the powers of sin to corrupt and torment. More and more we see the reality of this description: "Wherefore, men are free according to the flesh; and all things are given them which are expedient unto man. And they are free to choose liberty and eternal life, through the great Mediator of all men, or to choose captivity and death, according to the captivity and power of the devil; for he seeketh that all men might be miserable like unto himself" (2 Nephi 2:27).

The Master not only foresees perfectly the growing power of the opposing forces but also knows what it is like to be mortal. He knows what it is like to have the cares of life press upon us. He knows that we are to eat bread by the sweat of our brows, and of the cares, concerns, and even sorrows that come from the command to bring children to the earth. And He knows that both the trials we face and our human powers to deal with them ebb and flow.

He knows the mistake we can so easily make: to underestimate the forces working for us and to rely too much on our human powers. And so He offers us the covenant to "always remember Him" and the warning to "pray always" so that we will place our reliance on Him, our only safety. It is not hard to know what to do. The very difficulty of remembering always and praying always is a needed spur to try harder. The danger lies in delay or drift.

MOVE FORWARD SPIRITUALLY

Years ago, one of the things we taught people we met as missionaries was that they could either progress or fall back spiritually. We told them it was dangerous to think they could stand still. I remember feeling it was true, and yet I wondered why it was so.

Time has taught me. As the forces around us increase in intensity, whatever spiritual strength was once sufficient will not be enough. And whatever growth in spiritual strength we once thought was possible, greater growth will be made available to us. Both the need for spiritual strength and the opportunity to acquire it will increase at rates which we underestimate at our peril.

Time has also taught me something about the ebb and flow of our own powers and about how we may not notice that change. Not long ago one of my married sons and his wife and baby visited our home. They stayed in our basement guest room. He found there a daily journal I had kept as a young father. I had forgotten it was there and what it contained. At dinner my son began to recount what he had read there of my experiences with him and his brothers and of my straining to live a little better, to have the Atonement work more fully in my life, and to become what I needed to be. He had read of my working intensely and praying earnestly into the early hours of the morning.

Those of you who have served missions may have had similar experiences as you have come upon your missionary journals put away in a closet in your home. You may have read and felt a shock as you remembered how hard you worked, how constantly you thought of the Savior and His sacrifice for you and for those you tried to meet and teach, and how fervently and often you prayed. The shock may have come from realizing how much the cares of life had taken you from where you once were, so close to always remembering and always praying.

My message is a plea, a warning, and a promise: I plead with you to do with determination the simple things that will move you forward spiritually.

Start with remembering Him. You will remember what you know and what you love. The Savior gave us the scriptures, paid for by prophets at a price we cannot measure, so that we could know Him. Lose yourself in them. Decide now to read more, and more effectively than you have ever done before.

Last December I learned again the power that comes from trying harder to have the scriptures opened to our hearts. It began when I noticed the scriptures of a man sitting next to me in a meeting. He opened them as the discussion progressed, and I could see that he had marked them, as I had done, but with a difference. He had placed colored tags on the edges of pages, keyed to the colors with which he had marked the scriptures. I asked him after the meeting to tell me about it. He showed me the front of his scriptures where he had placed a typed page. On that page were topics about the gospel, each with a colored line under it. He had placed the corresponding colored markers on the edge of the scripture pages so that he could study all the scriptures that were helpful to him on a particular topic.

Within a day I had purchased an inexpensive set of scriptures. But it took more than a few days and more than a few prayers for me to know the topics that would open the scriptures anew for me. I chose the topics that would teach me of my call to be a witness of Jesus Christ. The first topic was the witness that Jesus Christ is the Son of God, the next was that He is risen, and the third was that He is the head of His Church.

I would not urge you to buy a new set of scriptures, nor to get colored tags and colored pencils, nor to choose the topics I chose. But I plead with you to return to the scriptures in some way that opens your mind and heart to be taught.

Many of the scriptures have become familiar to us. Yet in just a few weeks what I remembered about the Savior, and what I felt about Him, were enriched.

I began to read with purpose. Perhaps it was because of the Christmas season, perhaps it was because I wanted always to remember Him, but I found myself drawn to the accounts of His birth. I read again His words, spoken to a prophet named Nephi, recorded in the Book of Mormon, familiar to us all. And yet it seemed new to me:

> Behold, I come unto my own, to fulfil all things which I have made known unto the children of men from the foundation of the world, and to do the will, both of the Father and of the Son—of the Father because of me, and of the Son because of my flesh. And behold, the time is at hand, and this night shall the sign be given.
>
> And it came to pass that the words which came unto Nephi were fulfilled, according as they had been spoken; for behold, at the going down of the sun there was no darkness; and the people began to be astonished because there was no darkness when the night came. (3 Nephi 1:14–15.)

And then, because my mind was set to try to know more of Him, I noticed in my reading another scripture that had somehow never before caught my eye. It is in Zechariah, not a frequent stopping place unless you are on a search. Zechariah prophesied of the Second Coming of the Savior with these words: "But it shall be one day which shall be known to the Lord, not day, nor night: but it shall come to pass, that at evening time it shall be light" (Zechariah 14:7).

Later, as I had never done before, I felt that I saw in my mind and felt in my heart the fulfillment of Samuel the

Lamanite's prophecy that the sun would set without darkness (see Helaman 14:3–4). I saw it at His birth, as if I were somewhere among the people in those lands of promise. And I saw it as it will be when He comes to stand, in resurrected glory, on the Mount of Olives. The darkness will be dispelled when the promised Messiah comes with healing in His wings. Knowing how much I need that healing, my heart nearly bursts with joy and love for Him at the thought of that light. I believe I will never see the dawning of a new day, as the sun banishes the darkness, without the sight triggering love in my heart for Him.

ALWAYS REMEMBERING HIM

I have learned from that journey again through the scriptures and my increase in love for Him something about always remembering. Fathers and mothers who love their children already know it. It is this: The child may be absent. The cares of the day may be great. Yet love for the child can be ever present in the heart of the parent, coloring and shaping every word, every act, and every choice.

I don't know all that is meant by the following passage of scripture, but at least part of it is about the possibility of a change in our hearts—that our love of the Savior might always be there and growing: "But charity is the pure love of Christ, and it endureth forever; and whoso is found possessed of it at the last day, it shall be well with him. Wherefore, my beloved brethren, pray unto the Father with all the energy of heart, that ye may be filled with this love, which he hath bestowed upon all who are true followers of his Son, Jesus Christ; that ye may become the sons of God; that when he shall appear we shall be like him, for we shall see him as he is; that we may have this hope; that we may be purified even as he is pure" (Moroni 7:47–48).

Now I also plead with you to be determined to pray with all the energy of your heart that you might have every gift a loving Heavenly Father knows you must have to serve His Son and to endure against the powers of darkness.

PRAYERS OF THE HEART

Just as you can have love in your heart always, your heart can be drawn out in prayer always.

You remember that you were promised spiritual power, which can become greater in times of greater need. This is the Master's command through a prophet:

> Yea, humble yourselves, and continue in prayer unto him.
>
> Cry unto him when ye are in your fields, yea, over all your flocks.
>
> Cry unto him in your houses, yea, over all your household, both morning, mid-day, and evening.
>
> Yea, cry unto him against the power of your enemies.
>
> Yea, cry unto him against the devil, who is an enemy to all righteousness.
>
> Cry unto him over the crops of your fields, that ye may prosper in them.
>
> Cry over the flocks of your fields, that they may increase.
>
> But this is not all; ye must pour out your souls in your closets, and your secret places, and in your wilderness.
>
> Yea, and when you do not cry unto the Lord, let your hearts be full, drawn out in prayer unto him continually

for your welfare, and also for the welfare of those who are around you. (Alma 34:19–27.)

The Lord has given us touching evidence of the power of such prayers of the heart. The Book of Mormon tells of the people of Alma the Elder who would have been destroyed had they prayed openly:

> And Alma and his people did not raise their voices to the Lord their God, but did pour out their hearts to him; and he did know the thoughts of their hearts.
>
> And it came to pass that the voice of the Lord came to them in their afflictions, saying: Lift up your heads and be of good comfort, for I know of the covenant which ye have made unto me; and I will covenant with my people and deliver them out of bondage.
>
> And I will also ease the burdens which are put upon your shoulders, that even you cannot feel them upon your backs, even while you are in bondage; and this will I do that ye may stand as witnesses for me hereafter, and that ye may know of a surety that I, the Lord God, do visit my people in their afflictions.
>
> And now it came to pass that the burdens which were laid upon Alma and his brethren were made light; yea, the Lord did strengthen them that they could bear up their burdens with ease, and they did submit cheerfully and with patience to all the will of the Lord. (Mosiah 24:12–15.)

The Lord hears the prayers of your heart. The feelings in your heart of love for our Heavenly Father and for His Beloved Son can be so constant that your prayers will ascend always.

A WARNING

I must add to my pleading a warning. You have the right and the obligation to choose for yourselves. You can search the scriptures or not. You can choose to work hard enough, to ponder, and to obey His commandments so that the Holy Ghost can be your companion. Then you will come to know the Savior better and better and your heart will swell with love for Him. Or you can choose to delay. You can choose to drift, deciding past efforts will be enough.

My warning is a simple matter of cause and effect. Jesus Christ is the light and the life of the world. If we do not choose to move toward Him, we will find that we have moved away.

"For I the Lord cannot look upon sin with the least degree of allowance;

"Nevertheless, he that repents and does the commandments of the Lord shall be forgiven;

"And he that repents not, from him shall be taken even the light which he has received; for my Spirit shall not always strive with man, saith the Lord of Hosts" (D&C 1:31–33).

We are promised that if we always remember Him and keep His commandments, we will always have His Spirit to be with us. That light to our feet will grow dim if we choose to delay or to drift.

There is also a warning for us as we are faced with the choice of whether or not to try harder to have our hearts drawn out in prayer continually to God. Perhaps the thought will come into your mind that now is not the time to begin an earnest effort to pray with more faith. Or the thought may come that prayer is not important to you. You may know with certainty the source of such thoughts:

> And now, my beloved brethren, I perceive that ye ponder still in your hearts; and it grieveth me that I must speak concerning this thing. For if ye would hearken unto the Spirit which teacheth a man to pray ye would know that ye must pray; for the evil spirit teacheth not a man to pray, but teacheth him that he must not pray.
>
> But behold, I say unto you that ye must pray always, and not faint; that ye must not perform any thing unto the Lord save in the first place ye shall pray unto the Father in the name of Christ, that he will consecrate thy performance unto thee, that thy performance may be for the welfare of thy soul. (2 Nephi 32:8–9.)

PROMISES

Now for the sure promises. First, if you will let your heart be drawn to the Savior and always remember Him, and if you will draw near to our Heavenly Father in prayer, you will have put on spiritual armor. You will be protected against pride because you will know that any success comes not from your human powers. And you will be protected against the thoughts which come rushing in upon us that we are too weak, too inexperienced, too unworthy to do what we are called of God to do to serve and help save His children. We can have come into our hearts the reassurance recorded in Moroni: "And Christ truly said unto our fathers: If ye have faith ye can do all things which are expedient unto me" (Moroni 10:23).

There is another sure promise. It is this: Whether or not you choose to keep your covenant to always remember Him,

He always remembers you. I testify that Jesus Christ, born in Bethlehem, was and is the Only Begotten of the Father, the Lamb of God. He chose from before the foundations of the earth to be your Savior, my Savior, and the Savior of all we will ever know or meet. I testify that He was resurrected and that because of His Atonement we may be washed clean through our faith to obey the laws and accept the ordinances of the gospel.

I promise you that you will feel the influence of the Holy Ghost touch your heart as you search the scriptures with new purpose and as you pray earnestly. From that, you will have the assurance that God lives, that He answers prayers, that Jesus is the living Christ, and that He loves you. And you will feel your love for Him increase.

— 7 —

FINDING SAFETY
IN COUNSEL

The Savior has always been the protector of those who would accept His protection. He has said more than once, "How oft would I have gathered you as a hen gathereth her chickens, and ye would not" (3 Nephi 10:5).

The Lord expressed the same lament in our own dispensation after describing the many ways in which He calls us to safety: "How oft have I called upon you by the mouth of my servants, and by the ministering of angels, and by mine own voice, and by the voice of thunderings, and by the voice of lightnings, and by the voice of tempests, and by the voice of earthquakes, and great hailstorms, and by the voice of famines and pestilences of every kind, and by the great sound of a trump, and by the voice of judgment, and by the voice of mercy all the day long, and by the voice of glory and honor and the riches of eternal life, and would have saved you with an everlasting salvation, but ye would not!" (D&C 43:25).

There seems to be no end to the Savior's desire to lead us to safety. And there is constancy in the way He shows us the path. He calls by more than one means so that His call will

---

From a talk given at general conference, 5 April 1997.

reach those willing to accept it. And those means always include sending the message by the mouths of His prophets whenever people have qualified to have the prophets of God among them. Those authorized servants are always charged with warning the people, telling them the way to safety.

When tensions ran high in northern Missouri in the fall of 1838, the Prophet Joseph Smith called for all the Saints to gather to Far West for protection. Many were on isolated farms or in scattered settlements. He specifically counseled Jacob Haun, founder of a small settlement called Haun's Mill. A record of that time includes this: "Brother Joseph had sent word by Haun, who owned the mill, to inform the brethren who were living there to leave and come to Far West, but Mr. Haun did not deliver the message" (Philo Dibble, in "Early Scenes in Church History," in *Four Faith Promoting Classics* [Salt Lake City: Bookcraft, 1968], 90). Later, the Prophet Joseph recorded in his history: "Up to this day God had given me wisdom to save the people who took counsel. None had ever been killed who [had abided] by my counsel" (*History of the Church*, 2d ed., 7 vols. [Salt Lake City: Deseret Book Co., 1980], 5:137). Then the Prophet recorded the sad truth that innocent lives could have been saved at Haun's Mill had his counsel been received and followed.

In our own time, we have been warned with counsel of where to find safety from sin and from sorrow. One of the keys to recognizing those warnings is that they are repeated. For instance, more than once in general conference, you have heard our prophet say that he would quote a preceding prophet and would therefore be a second witness and sometimes even a third. Each of us who has listened has heard

President Kimball give counsel on the importance of a mother in the home and then heard President Benson quote him, and we have heard President Hinckley quote them both. The Apostle Paul wrote that "in the mouth of two or three witnesses shall every word be established" (2 Corinthians 13:1). One of the ways we may know that the warning is from the Lord is that the law of witnesses, authorized witnesses, has been invoked. When the words of prophets seem repetitive, that should rivet our attention and fill our hearts with gratitude to live in such a blessed time.

Looking for the path to safety in the counsel of prophets makes sense to those with strong faith. When a prophet speaks, those with little faith may think that they hear only a wise man giving good advice. Then if his counsel seems comfortable and reasonable, squaring with what they want to do, they take it. If it does not, they consider it either faulty advice or they see their circumstances as justifying their being an exception to the counsel. Those without faith may think that they hear only men seeking to exert influence for some selfish motive. They may mock and deride, as did a man named Korihor, with these words recorded in the Book of Mormon:

"And thus ye lead away this people after the foolish traditions of your fathers, and according to your own desires; and ye keep them down, even as it were in bondage, that ye may glut yourselves with the labors of their hands, that they durst not look up with boldness, and that they durst not enjoy their rights and privileges" (Alma 30:27).

Korihor was arguing, as men and women have falsely argued from the beginning of time, that to take counsel from the servants of God is to surrender God-given rights of independence. But the argument is false because it misrepresents reality. When we reject the counsel which comes from God, we do not choose to be independent of outside influence. We choose another influence. We reject the protection of a perfectly loving, all-powerful, all-knowing Father in Heaven, whose whole purpose, as that of His Beloved Son, is to give us eternal life, to give us all that He has, and to bring us home again in families to the arms of His love. In rejecting His counsel, we choose the influence of another power, whose purpose is to make us miserable and whose motive is hatred. We have moral agency as a gift of God. Rather than the right to choose to be free of influence, it is the inalienable right to submit ourselves to whichever of those powers we choose.

Another fallacy is to believe that the choice to accept or not accept the counsel of prophets is no more than deciding whether to accept good advice and gain its benefits or to stay where we are. But the choice not to take prophetic counsel changes the very ground upon which we stand. It becomes more dangerous. The failure to take prophetic counsel lessens our power to take inspired counsel in the future. The best time to have decided to help Noah build the ark was the first time he asked. Each time he asked after that, each failure to respond would have lessened sensitivity to the Spirit. And so each time his request would have seemed more foolish, until the rain came. And then it was too late.

Every time in my life when I have chosen to delay following inspired counsel or decided that I was an exception, I came to know that I had put myself in harm's way. Every time that I have listened to the counsel of prophets, felt it confirmed in prayer, and then followed it, I have found that I moved toward safety. Along the path, I have found that the way had been prepared for me and the rough places made smooth. God led me to safety along a path which was prepared with loving care, sometimes prepared long before.

The account at the beginning of the Book of Mormon is of a prophet of God, Lehi. He was also the leader of a family. He was warned by God to take those he loved to safety. Lehi's experience is a type of what happens as God gives counsel through His servants. Of Lehi's family, only those who had faith and who themselves received confirming revelation saw both the danger and the way to safety. For those without faith, the move into the wilderness seemed not only foolish but dangerous. Like all prophets, Lehi, to his dying day, tried to show his family where safety would lie for them.

He knew that the Savior holds responsible those to whom He delegates priesthood keys. With those keys comes the power to give counsel that will show us the way to safety. Those with keys are responsible to warn even when their counsel might not be followed. Keys are delegated down a line which passes from the prophet through those responsible for ever smaller groups of members, closer and closer to families and to individuals. That is one of the ways by which the Lord makes a stake a place of safety. For instance, I have sat with my wife in a meeting of parents called by our bishop, our neighbor, so that he could warn us of spiritual dangers faced by our children.

I heard more than the voice of my wise friend. I heard a servant of Jesus Christ, with keys, meeting his responsibility to warn and passing to us, the parents, the responsibility to act. When we honor the keys of that priesthood channel by listening and giving heed, we tie ourselves to a lifeline which will not fail us in any storm.

Our Heavenly Father loves us. He sent His Only Begotten Son to be our Savior. He knew that in mortality we would be in grave danger, the worst of it from the temptations of a terrible adversary. That is one of the reasons why the Savior has provided priesthood keys, so that those with ears to hear and faith to obey could go to places of safety.

Having listening ears requires humility. You remember the Lord's warning to Thomas B. Marsh. He was then the President of the Quorum of the Twelve Apostles. The Lord knew that President Marsh and his brethren of the Twelve would be tested. He gave counsel about taking counsel. The Lord said, "Be thou humble; and the Lord thy God shall lead thee by the hand, and give thee answer to thy prayers" (D&C 112:10).

The Lord added a warning that is applicable to any who follow a living prophet: "Exalt not yourselves; rebel not against my servant Joseph; for verily I say unto you, I am with him, and my hand shall be over him; and the keys which I have given unto him, and also to youward, shall not be taken from him till I come" (D&C 112:15).

God offers us counsel not just for our own safety but for the safety of His other children, whom we should love. There are few comforts so sweet as to know that we have been an instrument in the hands of God in leading someone else to safety. That blessing generally requires the faith to follow counsel when it is hard to do. An example from Church history is that of Reddick Newton Allred. He was one of the rescue party sent out by Brigham Young to bring in the Willie and Martin Handcart Companies. When a terrible storm hit, Captain Grant, captain of the rescue party, decided to leave some of the wagons by the Sweetwater River as he pressed ahead to find the handcart companies. With the blizzards howling and the weather becoming life-threatening, two of the men left behind at the Sweetwater decided that it was foolish to stay. They thought that either the handcart companies had wintered over somewhere or had perished. They decided to return to the Salt Lake Valley and tried to persuade everyone else to do the same.

Reddick Allred refused to budge. Brigham had sent them out and his priesthood leader had told him to wait there. The others took several wagons, all filled with needed supplies, and started back. Even more tragic, each wagon they met coming out from Salt Lake they turned back as well. They turned back seventy-seven wagons, returning all the way to Little Mountain, where President Young learned what was happening and turned them around again. When the Willie Company was finally found, and had made that heartrending pull up and over Rocky Ridge, it was Reddick Allred and his wagons that waited for them. (See Rebecca Bartholomew and Leonard J. Arrington, *Rescue of the 1856 Handcart Companies*, rev. ed. [Provo, Utah: Brigham Young University, Charles Redd Center for Western Studies, 1992], 29, 33–34.)

In general conferences you have heard inspired counsel, for instance, to reach out to the new members of the Church. Those with the faith of Reddick Newton Allred will keep offering friendship even when it seems not to be needed or to have no effect. They will persist. When some new member reaches the point of spiritual exhaustion, they will be there offering kind words and fellowship. They will then feel the same divine approval Brother Allred felt when he saw those handcart pioneers struggling toward him, knowing he could offer them safety because he had followed counsel when it was hard to do.

While the record does not prove it, I am confident that Brother Allred prayed while he waited. I am confident that his prayers were answered. He then knew that the counsel to stand fast was from God. We must pray to know that. I promise you answers to such prayers of faith.

Sometimes we will receive counsel that we cannot understand or that seems not to apply to us, even after careful prayer and thought. Don't discard the counsel, but hold it close. If someone you trusted handed you what appeared to be nothing more than sand with the promise that it contained gold, you might wisely hold it in your hand awhile, shaking it gently. Every time I have done that with counsel from a prophet, after a time the gold flakes have begun to appear and I have been grateful.

We are blessed to live in a time when the priesthood keys are on the earth. We are blessed to know where to look and how to listen for the voice that will fulfill the promise of the Lord that He will gather us to safety. I pray for you and for me that we will have humble hearts, that we will listen, that we will pray, that we will wait for the deliverance of the Lord, which is sure to come as we are faithful.

— 8 —

THAT WE MAY BE ONE

The Savior of the world, Jesus Christ, said of those who would be part of His Church: "Be one; and if ye are not one ye are not mine" (D&C 38:27). And at the creation of man and woman, unity for them in marriage was not given as hope, it was a command! "Therefore shall a man leave his father and his mother, and shall cleave unto his wife: and they shall be one flesh" (Genesis 2:24). Our Heavenly Father wants our hearts to be knit together. That union in love is not simply an ideal. It is a necessity.

The requirement that we be one is not for this life alone. It is to be without end. The first marriage was performed by God in the garden when Adam and Eve were immortal. He placed in men and women from the beginning a desire to be joined together as man and wife forever to dwell in families in a perfect, righteous union. He placed in His children a desire to live at peace with all those around them.

But with the Fall it became clear that living in unity would not be easy. Tragedy struck early. Cain slew Abel, his brother. The children of Adam and Eve had become subject

From a talk given at general conference, 5 April 1998.

to the temptations of Satan. With skill, hatred, and cunning, Satan pursues his goal. It is the opposite of the purpose of our Heavenly Father and the Savior. They would give us perfect union and eternal happiness. Satan, their enemy and ours, has known the plan of salvation from before the Creation. He knows that only in eternal life can those sacred, joyful associations of families endure. Satan would tear us from loved ones and make us miserable. And it is he who plants the seeds of discord in human hearts in the hope that we might be divided and separate.

All of us have felt something of both union and separation. Sometimes in families and perhaps in other settings we have glimpsed life when one person put the interests of another above his or her own, in love and with sacrifice. And all of us know something of the sadness and loneliness of being separate and alone. We don't need to be told which we should choose. We know. But we need hope that we can experience unity in this life and qualify to have it forever in the world to come. And we need to know how that great blessing will come so that we can know what we must do.

The Savior of the world spoke of that unity and how we will have our natures changed to make it possible. He taught it clearly in the prayer He gave in His last meeting with His Apostles before His death. That supernally beautiful prayer is recorded in the book of John. He was about to face the terrible sacrifice for all of us that would make eternal life possible. He was about to leave the Apostles, whom He had ordained, whom He loved, and with whom He would leave the keys to lead His Church. And so He prayed to His Father, the perfect Son to the perfect Parent. We see in His words the way families will be made one, as will all the children of our Heavenly Father who follow the Savior and His servants:

"As thou hast sent me into the world, even so have I also sent them into the world.

"And for their sakes I sanctify myself, that they also might be sanctified through the truth.

"Neither pray I for these alone, but for them also which shall believe on me through their word; that they all may be one; as thou, Father, art in me, and I in thee, that they also may be one in us: that the world may believe that thou hast sent me" (John 17:18–21).

In those few words He made clear how the gospel of Jesus Christ can allow hearts to be made one. Those who will believe the truth He taught can accept the ordinances and the covenants offered by His authorized servants. Then, through obedience to those ordinances and covenants, their natures will be changed. The Savior's Atonement in that way makes it possible for us to be sanctified. We can then live in unity, as we must to have peace in this life and to dwell with the Father and His Son in eternity.

The ministry of the apostles and prophets in that day, as it is today, was to bring the children of Adam and Eve to a unity of the faith in Jesus Christ. The ultimate purpose of what they taught, and of what we teach, is to unite families: husbands, wives, children, grandchildren, ancestors, and finally all of the family of Adam and Eve who will choose it.

You remember the Savior prayed, "For their sakes"—speaking of the Apostles—"I sanctify myself, that they also might be sanctified through the truth" (John 17:19). The

Holy Ghost is a sanctifier. We can have the Spirit as our companion because the Lord restored the Melchizedek Priesthood through the Prophet Joseph Smith. The keys of that priesthood are on the earth today. By its power we can make covenants which allow us to have the Holy Ghost constantly.

Where people have that Spirit with them, we may expect harmony. The Spirit puts the testimony of truth in our hearts, which unifies those who share that testimony. The Spirit of God never generates contention (see 3 Nephi 11:29). It never generates the feelings of distinctions between people which lead to strife (see Joseph F. Smith, *Gospel Doctrine*, 131). It leads to personal peace and a feeling of union with others. It unifies souls. A unified family, a unified Church, and a world at peace depend on unified souls.

Even a child can understand what to do to have the Holy Ghost as a companion. The sacramental prayer tells us. We hear it every week as we attend our sacrament meetings. In those sacred moments we renew the covenants we made at baptism. And the Lord reminds us of the promise we received as we were confirmed members of the Church—the promise that we might receive the Holy Ghost. Here are some of the words of the sacramental prayer: "They are willing to take upon them the name of thy Son, and always remember him and keep his commandments which he has given them; that they may always have his Spirit to be with them" (D&C 20:77).

We can have His Spirit by keeping that covenant. First, we promise to take His name upon us. That means we must see ourselves as His. We will put Him first in our lives. We will want what He wants rather than what we want or what the world teaches us to want. As long as we love the things of the world first, there will be no peace in us. Holding an ideal for a family or a nation of comfort through material goods will, at last, divide them (see Harold B. Lee, *Stand Ye in Holy Places* [Salt Lake City: Deseret Book Co., 1974], 97). The ideal of doing for each other what the Lord would have us do, which follows naturally from taking His name upon us, can take us to a spiritual level which is a touch of heaven on earth.

Second, we promise always to remember Him. We do that every time we pray in His name. Especially when we ask for His forgiveness, as we must do often, we remember Him. At that moment we remember His sacrifice that makes repentance and forgiveness possible. When we plead, we remember Him as our advocate with the Father. When the feelings of forgiveness and peace come, we remember His patience and His endless love. That remembering fills our hearts with love.

We also keep our promise to remember Him when as families we pray together. At family prayer around a breakfast table, one child may pray for another to be blessed that things will go well that day in a test or in some performance. When the blessings come, the child blessed will remember the love of the morning and the kindness of the Advocate in whose name the prayer was offered. Hearts will be bound in love.

We keep our covenant to remember Him every time we gather our families to read the scriptures. They testify of the Lord Jesus Christ, for that is the message and always has been of prophets. Even if children do not remember the words, they will remember the true Author, who is Jesus Christ.

Third, we promise as we take the sacrament to keep His commandments, all of them. President J. Reuben Clark Jr., as he pled—as he did many times—for unity in a general conference talk, warned us against being selective in what we will obey. He put it this way: "The Lord has given us nothing that is useless or unnecessary. He has filled the Scriptures with the things which we should do in order that we may gain salvation."

President Clark went on: "When we partake of the Sacrament we covenant to obey and keep his commandments. There are no exceptions. There are no distinctions, no differences" (in Conference Report, April 1955, 10–11). President Clark taught that just as we repent of all sin, not just a single sin, we pledge to keep all the commandments. Hard as that sounds, it is uncomplicated. We simply submit to the authority of the Savior and promise to be obedient to whatever He commands (see Mosiah 3:19). It is our surrender to the authority of Jesus Christ that will allow us to be bound as families, as a Church, and as the children of our Heavenly Father.

The Lord conveys that authority through His prophet to humble servants. That faith turns our call as a home teacher or a visiting teacher into an errand from the Lord. We go for Him, at His command. An ordinary man and a teenage junior companion go into homes expecting that the powers of heaven will help them assure that families are united and that there is no hardness, lying, backbiting, nor evil speaking. That faith—that the Lord calls servants—will help us ignore their limitations when they reprove us, as they will. We will see their good intent more clearly than their human limitations. We will be less likely to feel offense and more likely to feel gratitude to the Master who called them.

There are some commandments that, when broken, destroy unity. Some have to do with what we say and some with how we react to what others say. We must speak no ill of anyone. We must see the good in each other and speak well of each other whenever we can (see David O. McKay, in Conference Report, Oct. 1967, 4–11).

At the same time, we must stand against those who speak contemptuously of sacred things, because the certain effect of that offense is to offend the Spirit and so create contention and confusion. President Spencer W. Kimball showed the way to stand without being contentious as he lay on a hospital gurney and asked an attendant who, in a moment of frustration, took the name of the Lord in vain: "'Please! Please! That is my Lord whose names you revile.' There was a deathly silence, then a subdued voice whispered: 'I am sorry'" (*The Teachings of Spencer W. Kimball*, 198). An inspired, loving rebuke can be an invitation to unity. Failure to give it when moved upon by the Holy Ghost will lead to discord.

If we are to have unity, there are commandments we must keep concerning how we feel. We must forgive and bear no malice toward those who offend us. The Savior set the example from the cross: "Father, forgive them; for they know not what they do" (Luke 23:34). We do not know the hearts of those who offend us. Nor do we know all the sources of our own anger and hurt. The Apostle Paul was telling us how to love in a world of imperfect people, including ourselves, when he said, "Charity suffereth long, and is kind; charity envieth not; charity vaunteth not itself, is not puffed up, doth not behave itself unseemly, seeketh not her own, is not easily provoked, thinketh no evil" (1 Corinthians 13:4–5). And then he gave solemn warning against reacting to the fault of others and forgetting our own when he wrote, "For now we see through a glass, darkly; but then face to face: now I know in part; but then shall I know even as also I am known" (1 Corinthians 13:12).

The sacramental prayer can remind us every week of how the gift of unity will come through obedience to the laws and ordinances of the gospel of Jesus Christ. When we keep our covenants to take His name upon us, to remember Him always, and to keep all His commandments, we will receive the companionship of His Spirit. That will soften our hearts and unite us. But there are two warnings which must come with that promise.

First, the Holy Ghost remains with us only if we stay clean and free from the love of the things of the world. A choice to be unclean will repel the Holy Ghost. The Spirit only dwells with those who choose the Lord over the world. "Be ye clean" (3 Nephi 20:41; D&C 38:42) and love God with all your "heart, . . . might, mind, and strength" (D&C 59:5) are not suggestions but commandments. And they are necessary to the companionship of the Spirit, without which we cannot be one.

The other warning is to beware of pride. A unity which comes to a family or to a people softened by the Spirit will bring great power. With that power will come recognition from the world. Whether that recognition brings praise or envy, it could lead us to pride. That would offend the Spirit. There is a protection against pride, that sure source of disunity. It is to see the bounties which God pours upon us not only as a mark of His favor but as an opportunity to join with those around us in greater service. A man and his wife learn to be one by using their similarities to understand each other and their differences to complement each other in serving one another and those around them. In the same way, we can unite with those who do not accept our doctrine but share our desire to bless the children of our Heavenly Father.

We can become peacemakers, worthy to be called blessed and the children of God (see Matthew 5:9). Jesus Christ offers to all who will accept it the standard of peace.

— 9 —

A LAW OF
INCREASING RETURNS

I was riding in a car with a wise man a few years ago. We talked about some tragedies in lives of people we knew. Some had waited too long, missing the chance to act. And some had waited not long enough. He said quietly, more to himself than to me, "Timing is everything."

Ecclesiastes said, with an elegance that goes beyond poetry to frame our problem: "To every thing there is a season, and a time to every purpose under the heaven: A time to be born, and a time to die; a time to plant, and a time to pluck up that which is planted."

And then later: "A time to get, and a time to lose; a time to keep, and a time to cast away" (Ecclesiastes 3:1–2, 6).

Waiting for a harvest takes more judgment in life than it does in gardening. In your garden, you can tell if the seed sprouts. And even an amateur can tell when the corn or carrots are ready. But I remember a story told to me long ago, far from here, by a sad voice. I remember it, not because it was unique but because I have heard the same story told, again

---

From a talk given at a Brigham Young University fireside, 28 March 1982.

and again, about waiting or failing to wait. The details vary, but not the feeling of drama.

She said it happened on a summer Saturday afternoon. She was tired. Tired of being single. Tired of trying to be a faithful Latter-day Saint. Not so much tired of being kind and virtuous as tired of nothing good seeming to come of it. She'd not had a date in months.

She saw no prospect of even becoming friends with, let alone marrying, a man who shared her faith and ideals. In frustration she found herself deciding something. She decided that afternoon, consciously, that years of good works and restraint had produced too little and promised no more. She said to herself almost aloud, "Oh, what's the use?"

The phone rang. It was a man's voice, a man she knew. He lived in the same apartment building. He'd asked her out before. She'd refused because she was sure he'd expect her to compromise standards she'd preserved at great effort. But, almost as if directed by a scriptwriter, he called at that instant.

She didn't say, "Yes." She said, "I'll think about it." She thought about it. He called again. And finally, she repeated to herself, "Oh, what's the use?" She went. She found she had been right about his intentions. And in a choice about time and about waiting or not waiting, her life changed. So she will never know what might have been ahead on the path she'd decided wasn't worth the price; she knew quickly the other one was uphill, and a hard climb.

All of us make decisions every day, almost every hour, about whether it's worth it to wait. The hardest ones are where the waiting includes working. Does it make sense to keep working, to keep sacrificing, when nothing seems to be coming from the effort?

There's a young man in the mission field who's made that choice in the last month. I heard his story, but there must have been thousands of such choices made last month. His companion would have made Job's critical friends seem like the Three Nephites. Just living and working with his companion required more contribution than the young missionary had dreamed he was going to have to make. The mission president authorized them to stay in their apartment because wind brought the effective temperature to 80 degrees below zero. So the young man had to decide, "Shall we go out? We've been tracting and it's produced nothing. For what it would cost us, what would we get? We haven't got a contact, so we'd just be hitting doors." Well, they went. That's an odd investment decision, but they went. What they got was to meet one man, behind one of a hundred doors. In his letter about the man's baptism, my young friend said, "I've never been more happy in my life."

THE LAW OF THE HARVEST

We're talking about an application of the law of the harvest. Common sense tells you there is such a law, and so did the Savior and so have the prophets. Remember how Paul said it:

"*Be not deceived; God is not mocked: for whatsoever a man soweth, that shall he also reap.*

"*For he that soweth to his flesh shall of the flesh reap corruption; but he that soweth to the Spirit shall of the Spirit reap life everlasting*" (Galatians 6:7–8; emphasis added).

Here we're talking just about sowing to the Spirit. We're concerned with that long list of requirements and commandments you already know are essential along the way to eternal life. We're going to try to understand one universal challenge: How to keep waiting and working when the harvest seems delayed.

The most important fact to note is that crops, even the spiritual ones, are not all of one kind. There are early maturing varieties and late varieties. Maybe you've noticed in seed catalogs that one variety of corn can be harvested in less, sometimes nearly half, the time it takes for another to be ready. You may not pay attention to that, but I do because I've lived in Rexburg, Idaho. It freezes there just before the Fourth of July, and sometimes just after.

Efforts, spiritual or practical, don't all bear fruit in the same length of time. You know that, but you may not have noticed something about your behavior that makes sense only if most of your experience is with early crops. Those are the ones where effort produces fast results. What happens after the early harvest? Would you expect an intelligent person to keep cultivating a field that had already produced its crop and been cleared? No, at least not in the hope of getting more harvest.

Now, one trouble with most of our struggles is that you can't see the seeds and the crops clearly. And you may not know as much about maturation time. So, you have to make this decision frequently: "Has this effort yielded about all it's going to, or shall I keep working and waiting?"

Most people usually assume they are working with early crops. Think of the last time you went home teaching or

visiting teaching. Did you visit once, and late in the month—
or not at all? Or did you reach out with extra contacts, extra
love, and extra service? Think of the last Sunday School lesson you prepared. How many times did you rework it? Did
you try another approach to the subject once you felt you had
a workable plan? Did you read some additional chapters in
the scriptures, beyond those assigned? How much time did
you spend on that last lesson? Twenty minutes? An hour? A
day? Several days?

DIMINISHING RETURNS

The answers will vary, but not much. For most of you,
the best bet is that you stopped early. Why? Because you
understand something called the "law of diminishing
returns." Most of you use it when you cut a lawn. You cut it
in one direction, then may cut it in the other, to get it
smoother. But not many of you would cut it a third time.
Why? Because you'd say, "It isn't worth it. I've gotten about
all the smoothness I'm going to get. And more than that, cutting it a third time will take nearly as much time as it did the
first."

Most of us believe in the law of conservation of energy,
particularly our own. We treat most of our effort like planting
and harvesting an early crop. We expect early results with little
more to come from keeping up the effort after the first rush of
rewards.

That makes good sense for cutting lawns. And it makes
good sense for many other things. In fact, it makes sense for
so many that I think you may find it easy to say in your mind,
"I pity some of those people who just seem like losers, always

working and always waiting." Something going on in the world around you encourages, almost demands, that attitude.

THE LATE CROPS

Husbands, wives, parents, and even children are familiar with deciding, "Shall I keep giving when I'm getting so little?" Families may be the best place to find out how the world feels about working and waiting for late crops. Families require some of the toughest investment decisions of all. Statistics show clearly which way the decisions are going in this country. In 1945, half the people in America thought four or more children was the ideal number for a family to have. By 1980, only 16 percent thought so. From 1960 to 1977, it's estimated that the number of unmarried people living together doubled, from half a million to a million. That's a million people who are unwilling even to start the investment process in a family.

Most of you know what investments—and patience—are required to maintain virtue, serve an effective mission, or build an eternal family. But perhaps many of you haven't given enough attention to how much the world is moving away from the idea of delaying gratification long enough to do those things.

Here's some grim arithmetic to let you see it. An economist named Henry Kaufmann has added up the wealth in America and subtracted all the debt. In 1964, that showed us about $400 million in the hole. By 1980, the hole had increased, or, since it's a hole, I should say sunk, to $3 trillion Even if his figures overstate the problem, they make clear the direction we've chosen. That tells you something about how much more we're demanding to have our future now. One farmer heard those numbers and said, "Why, we've been eating our seed corn."

You shouldn't really be surprised to be living in an "I want it now" generation. A prophet, Peter, saw it long ago. He said, "There shall come in the last days scoffers, walking after their own lusts, and saying, Where is the promise of his coming? for since the fathers fell asleep, all things continue as they were from the beginning of the creation" (2 Peter 3:3-4).

You are believers, not scoffers. Yet the scoffers can be helpful, because they encourage you to get an answer to this question: "What am I willing to keep giving heart and soul for, when neither I nor the scoffers may see returns for a long, long time?" And when we decide there are potential rewards worth that commitment, you'll want answers to another question: "How can I keep myself working and waiting if the scoffers are loud and the delay long?"

There are spiritual crops that require months, years, and sometimes a lifetime of cultivation before the harvest. Among them are spiritual rewards you want most. That shouldn't surprise you. Common sense tells you that what matters most won't come easily. But there is another reason suggested in the scriptures. Remember this from the Book of Mormon?

"And now, I, Moroni, . . . would show unto the world that faith is things which are hoped for and not seen; wherefore, dispute not because ye see not, for ye receive no witness until after the trial of your faith" (Ether 12:6).

And from the Doctrine and Covenants:

"Ye cannot behold with your natural eyes, for the present time, the design of your God concerning those things which shall come hereafter, and the glory which shall follow after much tribulation.

"For after much tribulation come the blessings. Wherefore the day cometh that ye shall be crowned with much glory; the hour is not yet, but is nigh at hand" (D&C 58:3–4).

THE LAW OF INCREASING RETURNS

If you wanted to give this idea a name, you could call it "the law of increasing returns." The simple fact is that there is a God who wants us to have faith in Him. He knows that to strengthen faith we must use it. And so He gives us the chance to use it by letting some of the spiritual rewards we want most be delayed. Instead of first efforts yielding returns, with a steady decline, it's the reverse. First efforts, and even second efforts, seem to yield little. And then the rewards begin, perhaps much later, to grow and grow.

Most of us need encouragement to work and wait for rewards. But not everybody. I knew one man who lived his life pretty much as if everything he did was working on a late crop. He was my father. He died one Christmas after a life filled with getting rewards, from the National Medal of Science in this country to the Wolff Prize in Israel. But if you'd watched him in private, you would have seen some unusual behavior.

I remember him arm wrestling my Aunt Rose once. She was visiting us in New Jersey, and we'd driven to the ice cream store. You'll know how old I am when I say a cone cost a dime. Aunt Rose tried to pay for our cones. Dad wrestled her for it. I remember being afraid he'd break her arm. He was determined he'd give, not receive. And she was going to receive a broken arm if that's what it took. They laughed, but Dad won.

He won that fight all his life, giving more than he got. He taught every term in his years at the University of Utah, including summers. There was no extra pay. It wasn't even required as part of the job. I remember his trading a first-class ticket for tourist and sending the difference to the company that had provided the ticket. His life was to give first class but always take tourist. Why? I've got an idea. He believed in the law of increasing returns. Give more than you take; invest in the future; cast your bread upon the waters.

You might think he was extreme. He probably was. My guess is that he left more of everything of this world's goods than he consumed in a lifetime, despite all the awards heaped on him. I don't recommend that to you, partly because it might drive your spouse slightly bonkers. But there is a scripture about behavior like that. It's in Matthew 6:1–4:

> Take heed that ye do not your alms before men, to be seen of them: otherwise ye have no reward of your Father which is in Heaven.
>
> Therefore when thou doest thine alms, do not sound a trumpet before thee, as the hypocrites do in the synagogues and in the streets, that they may have glory of men. Verily I say unto you, They have their reward.
>
> But when thou doest alms, let not thy left hand know what thy right hand doeth:
>
> That thine alms may be in secret: and thy Father which seeth in secret himself shall reward thee openly.

I wouldn't suggest Dad fought to buy the ice cream because he wanted a reward in heaven. He just had a general bias toward putting in hard work up front and letting the rewards take a long time to come, even forever.

Even in the confusion of the last night I spent with him, he gave me some advice. I was helping him walk. I'm not even sure he knew I was there. But very clearly, almost with a booming voice, he said, "Well, let's just do the homework tonight, and we'll see how the exam goes in the morning." He's getting the grade now, and he spent a life doing as much homework as he could. Most of us could move profitably toward a little more homework, and leave the grades for tomorrow.

My guess is that all of us want to be better at working and waiting. Let me give you some advice about how to do it. It all follows from what we've said about the law of increasing returns, about planting and tending late crops. But it's not just theory. I got these hints from watching people who are the best I've seen at working and waiting on late crops. As the ads say, "This product has been proven in clinical tests."

All these hints have to do with where you focus your eyes. Two are things you ought to notice about the present, while you're working and waiting and not getting much yet in return. And the last two are ways to look at the glorious future you're working and waiting for.

See the Humor in Things

First, keep your eyes open for humor in the present. The people I know who are good for the long haul all seem to smile easily. It's not hard for me to understand, for instance, that the Prophet Joseph Smith, who marched triumphantly through trouble, would describe himself as having a "cheerful disposition." You can't just get yourself a cheerful disposition, but you could keep your eyes open for something to smile at.

It's not hard. That's because the best humor springs from seeing the incongruity in your own predicament. Who's got more predicament than someone giving lots with small result? And who's more apt to laugh easily at himself than someone who has ultimate faith that the predicament will end? So look for the chance to smile.

I've had some experience in the chain-saw business. One joke keeps reappearing with new variations. The father of them all goes like this: A customer bought his first chain saw. He was told how many trees he'd be able to cut an hour. He came back to the dealer complaining. He couldn't cut a tenth that many trees. The saw was checked and found perfect. He was reassured that practice and time would solve the problem. He kept coming back as many times as you want to extend the story to make it funny.

Finally, in desperation, the dealer said, "Let me take you out to the forest and show you." They got there, the dealer pulled the cord, the engine roared, and the customer said, "What's that?"

Many who hear that story laugh slowly or not at all. But try that story on a woodcutter. He pictures quickly that poor man sawing on a tree with a chain saw with the motor not running. You've got to know how heavy they are. You need to have cut down a tree. If you have, you roar. Why? Because it's funny to think of yourself flailing away. They even have an expression for it, when they're trying to persuade you of something and failing: "Well, I'm swinging the axe, but no chips are flying."

Most returned missionaries and most married couples have swung the axe and seen no chips flying. You could top, those of you who have been there, any funny story I'd try to tell. And if we were in a small group, you'd try. That's not because we are humorists. And it's not because missions or marriage or dedicated service are not serious. They are very serious. But the incongruities of giving more than you seem to get guarantee the chance to smile at yourself. I hope you will. All it will take is to keep your eyes open. And I think it's a key to endurance.

FOCUS ON YOUR BLESSINGS

The second place to focus your eyes is on the blessings you are getting now, while you wait. When you are trying hard to give, knowing the rewards will be delayed, it's terribly easy to overlook other blessings. Not all blessings are delayed. The early harvest is all around you. King Benjamin suggested you start by noticing that you are breathing. He also said, as you likely remember, "And secondly, he doth require that ye should do as he hath commanded you; for which if ye do, he doth immediately bless you; and therefore he hath paid you" (Mosiah 2:24).

Some results may be delayed to allow you to strengthen your faith. But other blessings come immediately. And King Benjamin valued those so highly compared to what we give that he said, "Mark your whole bill 'Paid in full.'" I know that's hard to do if you are struggling under a heavy load. It's easy to see your load and to pine for the delayed rewards. But King Benjamin taught us that we're already abundantly paid, both with free gifts—such as life, for which we have done nothing—and with other blessings which have followed immediately upon our faithful service.

Just that focus of the eyes might save your marriage someday. I'll guarantee you one thing. You won't contract a great marriage; you'll build one. Now that's not saying that some contracts to build aren't a lot better than others. But it will take effort and time. Maybe a lot of time. And millions of men and women every year, or day, or hour must mutter, "What am I getting out of this? If it weren't for the children—" Hold it right there: "The children."

Once Elizabeth, then two years old, saw the picture of her father in the paper. She said, "That's Dad. He wants to change with me." That doesn't mean much to you. In fact, it might even confuse you because you might not know she's talking about helping her father change himself, rather than having him change her clothes. Her statement means a lot to me because I'm the guy who sits on the floor when she says, "You sit here." I'll tell you something. All she has to do is hand me those shoe trees one time and then say, "Let me kiss your head" (which, as you may know, is easy to hit), and you can mark anything owed me on the marriage account, "Paid in full."

I recognize that's easy for a father to say. Mothers invest so much more in children that a kiss from a little girl still leaves a lot for the future. Men and women working outside the home deal mostly with early crops and with the law of diminishing returns. In the home, they spend far more on late crops and the law of increasing returns. It's important to remember that. It could help a woman understand why arguments for a career and little time spent rearing children are so tempting. And it might help a man understand why a child trampling on the teachings of the home may tear at his wife even more than at him. His paycheck comes often. Hers may come a few times in her life. And now perhaps, because of the choice of a child, one check may not come at all.

But for men and women, obsessed as they should be with the eternal results that take so long, it helps to see the blessings already in hand. The prettiest flowers I've ever seen were among rocks near the tops of mountains. That must have been partly because I worked so hard to get there—for something else—and then, suddenly, there they were. By forcing yourself to look at them, at the blessings around you, it will be easy to do what King Benjamin suggested: "O how you ought to thank your heavenly King!" (Mosiah 2:19).

Among the reasons we ought to be thankful is that it will improve our vision. And with an eye on today's blessings you'll have more staying power for the distant goal.

THE DISTANT GOAL

Now, let me suggest how to keep your eye on the distant goal. What will a successful mission look like? How can I picture a great marriage? Or what does a wonderful marriage look like in retirement years? That's hard to see before you get there. And it's hard to persevere without some picture.

I've never forgotten the sacrament meeting talk of an Englishman who had spent four years in a Japanese prison camp. Two missionaries had found and baptized him just before the capture of Singapore. He lost all his possessions save a photograph of the two missionaries. And that he kept hidden from his captors. He survived, he said, largely by finding moments, sometimes hidden under a blanket, when he could look at the picture and imagine himself talking to the elders again. So vivid is that evening sacrament meeting to me that I remember now, thirty-five years later, that he finished his testimony and sang "The Holy City."

You rarely can have a photograph of that future for which you now sacrifice, but you can get pictures. Years ago, near the time of that sacrament meeting, it occurred to me that I would sometime perhaps have a family. I even joked about them, calling them "the redheads." My mother's hair had been red when she was young. I certainly didn't think the idea of redheads was inspiration, just an idea. But more than once that picture was enough to make me work, and wait.

If all my four sons were here tonight, you would see two blond heads and two red ones. In a kitchen chat one evening, one of them said to me he'd not mind exchanging red hair for beach-boy blond. I just smiled. All dads may think their sons are handsome, but I would not exchange his red hair, nor my early vision of it, for spun gold.

It's not wise to daydream, and I'm not recommending it. If a girl dreams too much about a house or a car, some poor man will someday have to get it for her. But I do recommend a little thought, not about things or places, but about people. All the late crops, all the assignments God will reward in the long run that I can think of, involve serving someone else.

For example, now and then I try to think of my children as parents, perhaps older than I am now, perhaps at the end of their lives.

I learned something about the end of life from watching

my father at the end of his. He talked a lot about his father. His father was kind. His father believed in him. His father liked to be with him so much that he got him a horse to ride the range with him before my dad could walk. That's what he talked about at the end, when priorities got very clear. Perhaps much of what he did, in science, in serving God, was possible because of what his father did.

Just that little vision of the future makes me eager when the younger boys ask, "Dad, can we go to the Deseret Gym tonight?" and the older ones say, "Let's hit a few tennis balls." It's not quite the same as riding with your son on the Piedras Verdes, the way Grandpa did. But I hope it has just half the results.

I suppose those pictures are really visions. And you'd have to pray for them, or take them as gifts. But at least watch for them. You may catch glimmers. I have had a few. And they help.

DELAYED BLESSINGS

Now, finally, it's important to look carefully at those delayed blessings to notice that they are of at least two kinds. Some you can see and touch, and maybe even spend. You remember them.

For keeping the Sabbath day, long enough, the promise is: "Verily I say, that inasmuch as ye do this, the fulness of the earth is yours, the beasts of the field and the fowls of the air, and that which climbeth upon the trees and walketh upon the earth" (D&C 59:16).

There are many promises of tangible things. And you and I know of instances where faithful performance seems not to have yet produced the blessings. But for all sacred performances in serving God, there is another promised blessing. You couldn't touch it or spend it, and you can only see it with special vision. But I commend developing the skill to see it.

A man named Helaman had such skill. He was struggling under great uncertainty about what was ahead. He was working and waiting. Here's what he said happened: "Yea, and it came to pass that the Lord our God did visit us with assurances that he would deliver us; yea, insomuch that he did speak peace to our souls, and did grant unto us great faith, and did cause us that we should hope for our deliverance in him" (Alma 58:11).

If you learn how to see it, you can know that many people have had that peace spoken to their souls. There are men and women undergoing trials and tests of faith that might lead you to say, "Their faith will break." But it doesn't break, and they do take it. And if you will look carefully, you will realize that peace has been spoken to their souls and faith in deliverance increased. If you notice that, it will make it more likely that you will feel that peace. I bear you my testimony that you can.

I pray that you won't let the world nudge you toward spending your futures now. There are some things you should work for and expect results now. But along with getting early harvests, I hope you'll work and wait for the late ones. That will take seeing the law of increasing returns as an opportunity, not just a test. Delayed blessings will build your faith in God to work, and wait, for Him. The scriptures aren't demeaning when they command, "Wait upon the Lord" (Psalm 37:9; Isaiah 8:17; 40:31). That means both service and patience. And that will build your faith.

Leading
Others to
Christ

— 10 —

THE POWER OF
TEACHING DOCTRINE

There has been a war between light and darkness, between good and evil, since before the world was created. The battle still rages, and the casualties seem to be increasing. All of us have family members we love who are being buffeted by the forces of the destroyer, who would make all God's children miserable. For many of us, there have been sleepless nights. We have tried to add every force for good we can to the powers swirling around the people who are at risk. We have loved them. We have set the best example we could. We have pled in prayer for them. A wise prophet long ago gave us counsel about another force which we may at times underestimate and thus use too little.

Alma was the leader of a people faced with destruction by ferocious enemies. In the face of that danger, he could not do everything, so he had to choose. He could have built fortifications or created armaments or trained armies. But his only hope of victory was to get God's help, and for that he knew the people must repent. And so he chose to try one thing first: "And now, as the preaching of the word had a great

From a talk given at general conference, 4 April 1999.

tendency to lead the people to do that which was just—yea, it had had more powerful effect upon the minds of the people than the sword, or anything else, which had happened unto them—therefore Alma thought it was expedient that they should try the virtue of the word of God" (Alma 31:5).

The word of God is the doctrine taught by Jesus Christ and by His prophets. Alma knew that words of doctrine have great power. They can open the minds of people to see spiritual things not visible to the natural eye. And they can open the heart to feelings of the love of God and a love for truth. The Savior drew on both those sources of power, to open our eyes and open hearts, in the eighteenth section of the Doctrine and Covenants as He taught His doctrine to those whom He wants to serve Him as missionaries. As you read, think of that young man in your family now wavering in preparing himself for a mission. Here is how the Master taught two of His servants and how you might teach His doctrine to the young man you love:

"And now, Oliver Cowdery, I speak unto you, and also unto David Whitmer, by the way of commandment; for, behold, I command all men everywhere to repent, and I speak unto you, even as unto Paul mine apostle, for you are called even with that same calling with which he was called.

"Remember the worth of souls is great in the sight of God" (D&C 18:9–10).

He begins by saying how much He trusts them. Then He draws their hearts to Him by saying how much He and His Father love every soul. He next goes to the foundation of His doctrine. He describes how much we have cause to love Him:

"For, behold, the Lord your Redeemer suffered death in the flesh; wherefore he suffered the pain of all men, that all men might repent and come unto him.

"And he hath risen again from the dead, that he might bring all men unto him, on conditions of repentance.

"And how great is his joy in the soul that repenteth!" (D&C 18:11–13).

Having given the doctrine of His mission to open their hearts, He gives them His command: "Wherefore, you are called to cry repentance unto this people" (D&C 18:14).

Finally, He opens their eyes to see beyond the veil. He takes them and us to a future existence, described in the great plan of salvation, where we may yet be. He tells us of wonderful associations, worth giving our all to enjoy:

"And if it so be that you should labor all your days in crying repentance unto this people, and bring, save it be one soul unto me, how great shall be your joy with him in the kingdom of my Father!

"And now, if your joy will be great with one soul that you have brought unto me into the kingdom of my Father, how great will be your joy if you should bring many souls unto me!" (D&C 18:15–16).

In those few passages, He teaches doctrine to open our hearts to His love. And He teaches doctrine to open our eyes to see spiritual realities, invisible to any mind not illuminated by the Spirit of Truth.

The need to open eyes and hearts tells us how we must teach doctrine. Doctrine gains its power as the Holy Ghost confirms that it is true. We prepare those we teach, as best we can, to receive the quiet promptings of the still, small voice. That takes at least some faith in Jesus Christ. It takes at least some humility, some willingness to surrender to the Savior's will for us. The person you would help may have little of either, but you can urge that they desire to believe. More than that, you can take confidence from another of the powers of doctrine. Truth can prepare its own way. Simply hearing the words of doctrine can plant the seed of faith in the heart. And even a tiny seed of faith in Jesus Christ invites the Spirit.

We have more control over our own preparation. We feast on the word of God in the scriptures and study the words of the living prophets. We fast and pray to invite the Spirit for ourselves and the person we would teach.

Because we need the Holy Ghost, we must be cautious and careful not to go beyond teaching true doctrine. The Holy Ghost is the Spirit of Truth. His confirmation is invited by our avoiding speculation or personal interpretation. That can be hard to do. You love the person you are trying to influence. He or she may have ignored the doctrine they have been taught. It is tempting to try something new or sensational. But we invite the Holy Ghost as our companion when we are careful to teach only true doctrine.

One of the surest ways to avoid even getting near false doctrine is to choose to be simple in our teaching. Safety is gained by that simplicity, and little is lost. We know this because the Savior has told us to teach the most important doctrine to little children. Listen to His command: "And again, inasmuch as parents have children in Zion, or in any of her stakes which are organized, that teach them not to understand the doctrine of repentance, faith in Christ the

Son of the living God, and of baptism and the gift of the Holy Ghost by the laying on of the hands, when eight years old, the sin be upon the heads of the parents" (D&C 68:25).

We can teach even a child to understand the doctrine of Jesus Christ. It is therefore possible, with God's help, to teach the saving doctrine simply.

We have the greatest opportunity with the young. The best time to teach is early, while children are still immune to the temptations of their mortal enemy, and long before the words of truth may be harder for them to hear in the noise of their personal struggles.

A wise parent would never miss a chance to gather children together to learn of the doctrine of Jesus Christ. Such moments are so rare in comparison with the efforts of the enemy. For every hour the power of doctrine is introduced into a child's life, there may be hundreds of hours of messages and images denying or ignoring the saving truths.

The question should not be whether we are too tired to prepare to teach doctrine or whether it wouldn't be better to draw a child closer by just having fun or whether the child isn't beginning to think that we preach too much. The question must be, "With so little time and so few opportunities, what words of doctrine from me will fortify them against the attacks on their faith which are sure to come?" The words you speak today may be the ones they remember. And today will soon be gone.

The years pass, we teach the doctrine the best we can, and yet some still do not respond. There is sorrow in that. But there is hope in the scriptural record of families. Think of Alma the Younger and Enos. In their moments of crisis, they remembered the words of their fathers, words of the doctrine of Jesus Christ. It saved them. Your teaching of that sacred doctrine will be remembered.

Two doubts may creep into your mind. You may wonder if you know the doctrine well enough to teach it. And if you have already tried to teach it, you may wonder why you can't see much of the good effects.

In my own family there is a story of a young woman who had the courage to start to teach doctrine when she was only a new convert with little education. And the fact that the effects of her teaching haven't ended gives me patience to wait for the fruits of my own efforts.

Mary Bommeli was my great-grandmother. I never met her. Her granddaughter heard her tell her story and wrote it down.

Mary was born in 1830. The missionaries taught her family in Switzerland when she was twenty-four. She was still living at home, weaving and selling cloth to help support her family on their small farm. When the family heard the doctrine of the restored gospel of Jesus Christ, they knew it was true. They were baptized. Mary's brothers were called on missions, going without purse or scrip. The rest of the family sold their possessions to go to America to gather with the Saints.

There was not enough money for all to go. Mary volunteered to stay behind because she felt she could earn enough from her weaving to support herself and save for her passage. She found her way to Berlin and to the home of a woman who hired her to weave cloth for the family's clothing. She lived in a servant's room and set up her loom in the living area of the home.

It was against the law then to teach the doctrine of The Church of Jesus Christ of Latter-day Saints in Berlin. But Mary could not keep the good news to herself. The woman of the house and her friends would gather around the loom to hear the Swiss girl teach. She talked about the appearance of Heavenly Father and Jesus Christ to Joseph Smith, of the visitation of angels, and of the Book of Mormon. When she came to the accounts of Alma, she taught the doctrine of the resurrection.

That caused some problems with her weaving. In those days, many children died very young. The women around the loom had lost children in death, some of them several children. When Mary taught the truth that little children were heirs of the celestial kingdom and that those women might again be with them and with the Savior and our Heavenly Father, tears rolled down the faces of the women. Mary cried too. All those tears falling got the cloth wet that Mary had woven.

Mary's teaching created a more serious problem. Even though Mary begged the women not to talk about what she told them, they did. They shared the joyous doctrine with their friends. So one night there was a knock at the door. It was the police. They took Mary off to jail. On the way, she asked the policeman for the name of the judge she was to appear before the next morning. She asked if he had a family. She asked if he was a good father and a good husband. The policeman smiled as he described the judge as a man of the world.

At the jail, Mary asked for a pencil and some paper. She wrote a letter to the judge. She wrote about the resurrection of Jesus Christ as described in the Book of Mormon, about the spirit world, and about how long the judge would have to think and to consider his life before facing the final judgment. She wrote that she knew he had much to repent of which would break his family's heart and bring him great sorrow. She wrote through the night. In the morning she asked the policeman to take her letter to the judge. He did.

Later, the policeman was summoned by the judge to his office. The letter Mary had written was irrefutable evidence that she was teaching the gospel and so breaking the law. Nevertheless, it wasn't long until the policeman came back to Mary's cell. He told her that all charges were dismissed and that she was free to go, on the conditions she had stated in her letter. Her teaching the doctrine of the restored gospel of Jesus Christ had opened eyes and hearts enough to get her cast into jail. And her declaring the doctrine of repentance to the judge got her cast out of jail (see Theresa Snow Hill, *Life and Times of Henry Eyring and Mary Bommeli* [Logan, Utah: T. S. Hill, 1997], 15–22).

The teaching of Mary Bommeli touched more than the judge and those women around the loom. My father, her grandson, talked to me during the nights as he approached death. He spoke of joyous reunions that were coming soon in the spirit world. I could almost see the bright sunlight and the smiles in that place of paradise as he talked about it with such assurance.

At one point, I asked him if he had some repenting to do. He smiled. He chuckled softly as he said, "No, Hal, I've been repenting as I went along." The doctrine of paradise that Mary Bommeli taught those women was real to her grandson. And even the doctrine Mary taught the judge had shaped my father's life for good. That will not be the end of Mary Bommeli's teaching. The record of her words will send true doctrine to generations of her family yet unborn. Because she believed that even a new convert knew enough doctrine to teach it, the minds and hearts of her descendants will be opened, and they will be strengthened in the battle.

Your descendants will teach doctrine to each other because you taught it. Doctrine can open more than minds to spiritual things and hearts to the love of God. When that doctrine brings joy and peace, it also has the power to open mouths. Like those women in Berlin, your descendants will not be able to keep the good news to themselves.

I am grateful to live in a time when we and our families have the fulness of the gospel restored. I am grateful for the Savior's mission of love for us and for the words of life which He has given us. I pray that we may share those words with those we love.

— 11 —

"A Voice of Warning"

Because the Lord is kind, He calls servants to warn people of danger. That call to warn is made harder and more important by the fact that the warnings of most worth are about dangers that people don't yet think are real. Think of Jonah. He fled at first from the call of the Lord to warn the people of Nineveh who were blinded to the danger by sin. He knew that wicked people through the ages have rejected prophets and sometimes killed them. Yet when Jonah went forward with faith, the Lord blessed him with safety and success.

We can also learn from our experiences as parents and as children. Those of us who have been parents have felt the anxiety of sensing danger our children cannot yet see. Few prayers are so fervent as those of a parent asking to know how to touch a child to move away from danger. Most of us have felt the blessing of hearing and heeding the warning voice of a parent.

I can still remember my mother speaking softly to me one Saturday afternoon when, as a little boy, I asked her for

From a talk given at general conference, 3 October 1998.

permission to do something I thought was perfectly reasonable and which she knew was dangerous. I still am amazed at the power she was granted, I believe from the Lord, to turn me around with so few words. As I remember them, they were: "Oh, I suppose you *could* do that. But the *choice* is yours." The only warning was in the emphasis she put on the words *could* and *choice*. Yet that was enough for me.

Her power to warn with so few words sprang from three things I knew about her. First, I knew she loved me. Second, I knew she had already done what she wanted me to do and been blessed by it. And third, she had conveyed to me her sure testimony that the choice I had to make was so important that the Lord would tell me what to do if I asked Him. Love, example, and testimony: those were keys that day, and they have been whenever I have been blessed to hear and then heed the warning of a servant of the Lord.

Our ability to touch others with our warning voice matters to all who are covenant disciples of Jesus Christ. Here is the charge given to each of the members of The Church of Jesus Christ of Latter-day Saints: "Behold, I sent you out to testify and warn the people, and it becometh every man who hath been warned to warn his neighbor" (D&C 88:81).

That command and warning of danger was given to those called as missionaries at the start of the Restoration. But the duty to warn our neighbor falls on all of us who have accepted the covenant of baptism. We are to talk with nonmember friends and relatives about the gospel. Our purpose is to invite them to be taught by the full-time missionaries who are called and set apart to teach. When a person has chosen to accept our invitation to be taught, a "referral" of great promise has been created, one far more likely to enter the waters of baptism and then to remain faithful.

As a member of the Church, you can expect that the full-time or the ward missionaries will ask for the opportunity to visit with you in your home. They will help you make a list of people with whom you could share the gospel. They may suggest you think of relatives, neighbors, and acquaintances. They may ask you to set a date by which you will try to have the person or family prepared to be taught, perhaps even ready to invite the missionaries. I've had that experience. Because we in our family accepted that invitation from the missionaries, I was blessed to perform the baptism of a widow in her eighties, taught by sister missionaries.

When I placed my hands on her head to confirm her a member of the Church, I felt impressed to say that her choice to be baptized would bless generations of her family, after and before her. She's dead now, but in a few weeks I will be in the temple with her son as he is sealed to her.

You may have had such experiences with people you have invited to be taught, and so you know that few moments in life are sweeter. The Lord's words are true for the missionaries and for all of us: "And now, if your joy will be great with one soul that you have brought unto me into the kingdom of my Father, how great will be your joy if you should bring many souls unto me!" (D&C 18:16).

The missionaries will help and encourage us, but whether such moments at the baptismal font and in the temple come more often will depend largely on how we see our charge and what we choose to do about it. The Lord would not use the word *warn* if there is no danger. Yet not many people we know sense it. They have learned to ignore the increasing evidence that society is unraveling and that their lives and family lack the peace they once thought was possible. That willingness to ignore the signs of danger can make it easy for you to think: *Why should I speak to anyone about the gospel who seems content? What danger is there to them or to me if I do or say nothing?*

Well, the danger may be hard to see, but it is real, both for them and for us. For instance, at some moment in the world to come, everyone you will ever meet will know what you know now. They will know that the only way to live forever in association with our families and in the presence of our Heavenly Father and His Son, Jesus Christ, was to choose to enter into the gate by baptism at the hands of those with authority from God. They will know that the only way families can be together forever is to accept and keep sacred covenants offered in the temples of God on this earth. And they will know that you knew. And they will remember whether you offered them what someone had offered you.

It's easy to say, "The time isn't right." But there is danger in procrastination. Years ago I worked for a man in California. He hired me, he was kind to me, he seemed to regard me highly. I may have been the only Latter-day Saint he ever knew well. I don't know all the reasons I found to wait for a better moment to talk with him about the gospel. I just remember my feeling of sorrow when I learned, after he had retired and I lived far away, that he and his wife had been killed in a late night drive to their home in Carmel, California. He loved his wife. He loved his children. He had loved his parents. He loved his grandchildren, and he will love their children and will want to be with them forever.

Now, I don't know how the crowds will be handled in the world to come. But I suppose that I will meet him, that he will look into my eyes, and that I will see in them the question: "Hal, you knew. Why didn't you tell me?"

When I think of him, and when I think of that widow I baptized and her family who will now be sealed to her and to each other, I want to do better. I want to increase my power to invite people to be taught. With that desire and with faith that God will help us, we will do better. It isn't hard to see how.

Love always comes first. A single act of kindness will seldom be enough. The Lord described the love we must feel, and that those we invite must recognize in us, with words like these: "Charity suffereth long," and it "beareth all things, believeth all things, hopeth all things, endureth all things" (1 Corinthians 13:4, 7).

I've seen what "suffereth long" and "endureth all things" mean. A family moved into a house near us. The home was new, so I was part of the crew of Latter-day Saints who spent a number of nights putting in landscaping. I remember the last night, standing next to the husband of the family as we finished. He surveyed our work and said to us standing nearby, "This is the third yard you Mormons have put in for us, and I think this is the best." And then he quietly but firmly told me of the great satisfaction he got from membership in his own church, a conversation we had often in the years he lived there.

In all that time, the acts of kindness extended to him and

his family never ceased because the neighbors really came to love them. One evening, I came home to see a truck in his driveway. I had been told they were moving to another state. I approached to see if I could help. I didn't recognize the man I saw loading household things into the truck. He said quietly as I drew near, "Hello, Brother Eyring." I hadn't recognized him because he was the son, now grown older, who had lived there, married, and moved away. And because of the love of many for him, he was now a baptized member of the Church. I don't know the end of that story because it will have no end. But I know that it begins with love.

Second, we will need to be better examples of what we invite others to do. In a darkening world, this command of the Savior will become more important: "Let your light so shine before men, that they may see your good works, and glorify your Father which is in heaven" (Matthew 5:16).

Most of us are modest enough to think that our small candle of example might be too dim to be noticed. But you and your family are watched more than you may realize. I had the chance in the spring of this year to attend and speak at meetings with nearly three hundred ministers and leaders of other churches. I visited alone with as many as I could. I asked them why they had been so attentive to my message, which was to recount the origins of the Church, to tell of the young Joseph Smith's First Vision and of living prophets. In every case, they gave essentially the same answer. They told a story of a person or a family—a story of knowing some of you. One repeated often was of a neighbor family, Latter-day Saints: "They were the finest family I have ever known." Often they spoke of some community effort or public response to a disaster where members of the Church worked in a way which to them seemed remarkable.

The people I met at those meetings could not yet recognize the truth in the doctrine, but they had already seen its fruit in your lives, and so they were ready to listen. They were ready to listen to the truths of the Restoration—that families can be sealed forever and that the gospel can change our very natures. They were ready because of your examples.

The third thing we must do better is to invite with testimony. Love and example will open the way. But we still have to open our mouths and bear testimony. We are helped by a simple fact. Truth and choice are inseparably connected. For everyone, there are some choices we must make to qualify for a testimony of spiritual truths. And for everyone, once we know a spiritual truth we must choose whether we will conform our lives to it. That means there are some things we must do before we invite our friends to make choices. And when we bear testimony of truth to them, we must convey to them the choices which, once they know that truth, they must make. There are two important examples: inviting someone to read the Book of Mormon and inviting someone to agree to be taught by the missionaries.

For us to know that the Book of Mormon is true, we must read it and make the choice found in Moroni: pray to know if it is true. When we have done that, we can testify from personal experience to our friends that they can make that choice and know the same truth. When they know the Book of Mormon is the word of God, they will face another choice: whether to accept your invitation to be taught by the missionaries. To make that invitation with testimony, you will need to know that the missionaries are called as servants of God.

You can gain that testimony by choosing to invite the missionaries into your home to teach your family or friends. Missionaries will welcome the opportunity. When you sit with them as they teach, as I have, you will know they are inspired with power beyond their years and their education. Then, when you invite others to choose to be taught by the missionaries, you will be able to bear testimony that they will teach the truth and that they offer the choices which lead to happiness.

Perhaps some of us may find it hard to believe that we love enough, or that our lives are good enough, or that our power to testify is sufficient for our invitations to our neighbors to be accepted. But the Lord knew we might feel that way. Listen to His encouraging words, which He directed to be placed at the first of the Doctrine and Covenants, when He gave us our charge: "And the voice of warning shall be unto all people, by the mouths of my disciples, whom I have chosen in these last days" (D&C 1:4).

And then, listen to His description of the qualifications of those disciples—of us: "The weak things of the world shall come forth and break down the mighty and strong ones" (D&C 1:19).

And then later, "That the fulness of my gospel might be proclaimed by the weak and the simple unto the ends of the world" (D&C 1:23).

And then again, "And inasmuch as they were humble

they might be made strong, and blessed from on high" (D&C 1:28).

That assurance was given to the first missionaries in the Church and to missionaries today. But it is given to all of us as well. We must have the faith that we can love enough and that the gospel has touched our lives enough that our invitation to choose can be heard as coming from the Master whose invitation it is.

His is the perfect example for what we are to do. You have felt His love and His caring, even when you did not respond, as those you approach with the gospel may not respond. Time after time He has invited you to be taught by His servants. You may not have recognized that in the visits of home teachers and visiting teachers or in a bishop's phone call, but those were His invitations to be helped and taught. And the Lord has always made consequences clear and then allowed us to choose for ourselves.

His servant Lehi taught his sons what has always been true for all of us: "And now, my sons, I would that ye should look to the great Mediator, and hearken unto his great commandments; and be faithful unto his words, and choose eternal life, according to the will of his Holy Spirit" (2 Nephi 2:28).

And then from Jacob this encouragement to meet your obligation to testify, as you must, that the choice to be taught by the missionaries is to enter the way toward eternal life, the greatest of all the gifts of God: "Therefore, cheer up your hearts, and remember that ye are free to act for yourselves— to choose the way of everlasting death or the way of eternal life" (2 Nephi 10:23).

I testify that only accepting and living the restored gospel of Jesus Christ brings the peace the Lord promised in this life and the hope of eternal life in the world to come. I testify that we have been given the privilege and the obligation to offer the truth and the choices which lead to those blessings to our Heavenly Father's children, who are our brothers and our sisters.

— 12 —

WITNESSES FOR GOD

The Latter-day Saints are a covenant people. From the day of baptism through the spiritual milestones of our lives, we make promises with God and He makes promises with us. He always keeps His promises offered through His authorized servants, but it is the crucial test of our lives to see if we will make and keep our covenants with Him.

I saw again the power of keeping covenants through a chance conversation with a man I sat down next to on a trip. I had never met him before, but apparently he had seen me in the crowd because his first words after I introduced myself were, "I've been watching you." He told me about his work. I told him about mine. He asked about my family, and then he told me something about his. He said that his wife was a member of the Church and that he was not.

After he came to trust me, he said something like this: "You know, there is something in your church you should fix. You need to tell your people when to quit." He explained that he and his wife had been married for twenty-five years. She

From a talk given at general conference, 5 October 1996.

had been a member of the Church since childhood. In their years of marriage she had only once stepped into a building of the Church, and that was to tour a temple before its dedication, and then only because her parents had arranged it.

Then, he told me why he thought we ought to make a change. He said that in those twenty-five years of married life, in which his wife showed no interest in the Church, visiting teachers and home teachers had never stopped coming to their home. He told of one evening when he went out to walk his dog alone only to find the home teacher happening by with his dog, eager to visit with him.

He told, with a touch of exasperation, of another night when he came home from a long business trip, put his car in the garage, and then came out to find his home teachers standing there, smiling. He said to me something like, "And there they were, right in my face, with another plate of cookies."

I think I understood his feelings. And then I tried, as best I could, to tell him how hard it would be to teach such teachers to quit. I told him that the love that he had felt from those many visitors and their constancy over the years in the face of little response came from a covenant they had made with God. I told him about the baptismal covenant as Alma described it in the Book of Mormon. I didn't quote these words, but you will remember them as Alma asked those he had taught whether they wished to be baptized:

> And it came to pass that he said unto them: Behold, here are the waters of Mormon (for thus were they called) and now, as ye are desirous to come into the fold of God,

and to be called his people, and are willing to bear one another's burdens, that they may be light;

Yea, and are willing to mourn with those that mourn; yea, and comfort those that stand in need of comfort, and to stand as witnesses of God at all times and in all things, and in all places that ye may be in, even until death, that ye may be redeemed of God, and be numbered with those of the first resurrection, that ye may have eternal life. (Mosiah 18:8–9.)

Those home teachers and visiting teachers understood and believed that the covenant to be a witness and to love were intertwined and that they reinforced each other. There is no other way to explain what had happened. My new friend recognized that the visitors had genuine concern for him and for his wife. And he knew their caring sprang from a belief that impelled them to come back. He seemed, at least to me, to understand that those visitors were driven from within by a covenant they would not break. As we parted I think he knew why he could expect that there would be more visits, more evidence of caring, and more patient waiting for the opportunity to bear testimony of the restored gospel. As we parted, I realized that I had learned something too. I will never again see home teaching or visiting teaching as only programs of the Church. Those faithful teachers saw what they were doing for what it really was. Such work is an opportunity, not a burden.

Every member has made the covenant in the waters of baptism to be a witness for God. Every member has made a covenant to do works of kindness as the Savior would do. So any call to bear witness and to care for others is not a request for extra service; it is a blessing designed by a loving Heavenly

Father and His Son, Jesus Christ. They have provided such calls as well as other settings, sometimes without a formal call, all for the same purpose. Each is a chance to prove what blessings flow from being a covenant people, and each is an opportunity for which you agreed to be accountable. Each is a sacred responsibility for others accepted in the waters of baptism but too often not met because it may not be recognized for what it is.

The power of that covenant to love and to witness should transform what members do in other settings across the world. One of the most important is in the family. Prophets in our time have consolidated our meetings on Sunday to allow time for families to be together. The prophets have also been inspired to help us reserve Monday night for family home evenings. Those opportunities require choices. In thousands of homes the choices made are guided by the covenant to comfort those that stand in need of comfort and to stand as witnesses of God.

Both the consolidation of the Sunday meetings and the creation of a family home evening are to provide opportunity for families to have time together to give Christlike service and to study the scriptures and gospel principles. The power of that possibility was taught by President Spencer W. Kimball this way: "I wonder what this world would be like if every father and mother gathered their children around them at least once a week, explained the gospel, and bore fervent testimonies to them. How could immorality continue and infidelity break families and delinquency spawn?" (*The Teachings of Spencer W. Kimball*, 345).

There are in those hours on Sunday and in a family home

evening on Monday the opportunity to combine genuine caring, teaching the gospel, and the bearing of testimony. Across the earth there are families who love and understand their covenants who do that. From my front window I have seen parents, their children at their sides, move down the street to the home of a neighbor to offer comfort, to give Christlike service. I wasn't there to see it, but surely the warmth of those moments lingered later at home when a song of Zion was sung, a prayer given that likely included a plea for the person visited, a scripture read, a short lesson taught, and testimonies of the restored gospel borne.

There is a caution I would give and a promise I would offer about such choices of how to use family time. For a person not yet a member of the Church, to fail to provide such moments of love and faith is simply a lost opportunity. But for those under covenant, it is much more. There are few places where the covenant to love and to bear witness is more easily kept than in the home. And there are few places where it can matter more for those for whom we are accountable. For members of the Church, my caution is that to neglect those opportunities is a choice not to keep sacred covenants.

Because God always honors covenants, I can make a promise to those who in faith keep the covenant to create experiences of giving love and bearing testimony with their families. They will reap a harvest of hearts touched, faith in Jesus Christ exercised unto repentance, and the desire and the power to keep covenants strengthened.

There is another circumstance in which the covenant to combine kindness with bearing witness has great power to change lives. Thousands of times every day members of the

Church are watched, as I was by the man I met on a trip, by people curious to know something about our lives. Because we are under covenant to be a witness, we will try to tell them how the gospel has brought us happiness. What they think of what we say may depend largely on how much they sense we care for them.

That was true when King Lamoni met Ammon, as we have it described in the Book of Mormon. Ammon had been captured by guards and brought to the king, who could take his life. But apparently within minutes King Lamoni recognized that Ammon cared enough for him to want to serve him. Ammon said, when offered high station, "Nay, but I will be thy servant" (Alma 17:25). Within days the king knew that Ammon was willing to risk his life for him. And then came the opportunity for Ammon to be a witness of God to the king.

Those we meet will feel the love that springs from our long practice in keeping a covenant to "mourn with those that mourn; yea, and comfort those that stand in need of comfort" (Mosiah 18:9). It may not be in hours or days as it was for King Lamoni, but they will feel our love after testing our hearts. And when they find our concern sincere, the Holy Spirit can more easily touch them to allow us to teach and to testify, as it did for Ammon.

Again I have a caution and a promise. The caution is that sorrow will come from failure either to love or to bear witness. If we fail to feel and show honest concern for those we approach with the gospel, they will reasonably distrust our message. But if out of fear of rejection we fail to tell them what the gospel has meant in our lives and could mean in theirs, we will someday share their sorrow. Either in this life or in the life to come, they will know that we failed to share with them the priceless gift of the gospel. They will know that accepting the gospel was the only way for them to inherit eternal life. And they will know that we received the gospel with a promise that we would share it.

I can make two promises to those who offer the gospel to others. The first is that even those who reject it will someday thank us. More than once I have asked missionaries to visit friends far from where I lived, learned that the missionaries had been rejected, and then received a letter from my friend with words like this: "I was honored that you would offer to me something that I knew meant so much to you." If not in this life, such messages will be sent to us in the world to come when those we approached will know the truth and how much we cared for them. My second promise is that as you offer the gospel to others, it will go down more deeply into your own heart. It becomes the well of water springing up into eternal life for us as we offer it to others.

There is one other setting which provides a near-perfect opportunity to combine love and testimony. In every ward and branch in the Church, once a month we hold a fast and testimony meeting. We fast for two meals. With the money saved, and adding more to it whenever we can, we pay a generous fast offering. The bishop and the branch president use those offerings, under inspiration, to care for the poor and the needy. Thus, by paying a fast offering we give comfort to those in need of comfort as we promised that we would.

The fast also helps us to feel humble and meek so that the Holy Ghost may more easily be our companion. By our fast, we both keep our covenant to care for others and we prepare to keep our covenant to bear testimony.

Those who have prepared carefully for the fast and testimony meeting won't need to be reminded how to bear testimony should they feel impressed to do it in the meeting. They won't give sermons or exhortations or travel reports or try to entertain as they bear witness. Because they will have already expressed appreciation to people privately, they will have less need to do it publicly. Neither will they feel a need to use eloquent language or to go on at length.

A testimony is a simple expression of what we feel. The member who has fasted both for the blessing of the poor and for the companionship of the Spirit will be feeling gratitude for the love of God and the certainty of eternal truth. Even a child can feel such things, which may be why sometimes the testimony of a child so moves us and why our preparation of fasting and prayer produces in us childlike feelings.

That preparation for the fast and testimony meeting is a covenant obligation for members of the Church. The offering of the gospel to those we meet and to our families are covenant obligations. We can take heart that our honest effort to keep our covenants allows God to increase our power to do it. We all need that assurance at times when our promise to love and to witness seems hard for us.

The fruit of keeping covenants is the companionship of the Holy Ghost and an increase in the power to love. That happens because of the power of the Atonement of Jesus Christ to change our very natures. We are eyewitnesses of that miracle of greater spiritual power coming to those who accept covenants and keep commandments. For instance, there are families across the Church who read and reread letters from their missionary children with wonder, and a few tears, at the miracle that in so short a time they have become new, better people.

Yet I have also seen that same miracle in a mature man and woman, called to serve as proselyting missionary companions in the most difficult of circumstances which would have taxed the bravest youth. As the husband made his report, I thought back to the man I had known. I realized that the promised miracle of spiritual growth is not a product of youth but of the faith simply to try to keep covenants. That couple went out to love the people and to bear witness, and they returned transformed as much as any twenty-one year old.

Each of us who have made covenants with God faces challenges unique to us. But each of us shares some common assurances. Our Heavenly Father knows us and our circumstances and even what faces us in the future. His Beloved Son, Jesus Christ, our Savior, has suffered and paid for our sins and those of all the people we will ever meet. He has perfect understanding of the feelings, the suffering, the trials, and the needs of every individual. Because of that, a way will be prepared for us to keep our covenants, however difficult that may now appear, if we go forward in faith.

I share with you the obligation to be a witness for God at all times and in all places that I will be in as long as I live. And I share with you the confidence that God can grant us the power to keep all our covenants.

— 13 —

TRUE FRIENDS

Each year, hundreds of thousands of the children of our Heavenly Father come into The Church of Jesus Christ of Latter-day Saints. For most it requires a great change in their lives. All of them have made a sacred covenant with great promises and with a solemn pledge to endure. That covenant is so important that our Heavenly Father described the blessing and the challenge to the prophet Nephi:

"And I heard a voice from the Father, saying: Yea, the words of my Beloved are true and faithful. He that endureth to the end, the same shall be saved.

"And now, my beloved brethren, I know by this that unless a man shall endure to the end, in following the example of the Son of the living God, he cannot be saved" (2 Nephi 31:15–16).

The Savior warns that if we start along the path and go far enough and then fail and deny Him, it would have been better if we had never begun (see 2 Nephi 31:14; D&C 40:1–3; 41:5–6).

From a talk given at general conference, 6 April 2002.

I think of that each time I visit with new members of the Church. I get that opportunity often, across the world. I see their trusting faces, and often they tell me about some trial of their faith, and then, with urgency in their voices, they whisper, "Please pray for me." At those moments, I feel again the weight of the charge to each of us from the Lord's living prophet. It is to keep the promise we made in the waters of baptism "to bear one another's burdens" (Mosiah 18:8). It is to be a friend.

These words of President Hinckley energize me: "I hope, I pray, I plead with you, every one of you, to embrace every new member of the Church. Make a friend of him or her. Hold onto them" (Meeting, Edmonton, Alberta, Canada, 2 Aug. 1998).

President Hinckley can't be there as a friend for every new member. But you can be there for at least one. All it takes is to feel something of what they feel and something of what the Savior feels for them. Try to feel the heart of a young man, Nkosiyabo Eddie Lupahla, in Africa, writing about his friend.

> Two and a half years prior to my joining the Church in 1999, my good friend, Mbuti Yona, looked me up. We had been friends through grades 5 to 12, then [were] separated when we attended different [schools].
>
> Mbuti was baptized in April 1999, and four weeks later he visited me at home and introduced the gospel to me. Regardless of the rumors about the Church, I was impressed by the "fellow Saints" who gave me a warm welcome on my first visit. It was this same Sunday that my friend introduced me to the missionaries. Arrangements were made to be taught. My friend was there for every

discussion, and he kept inviting me to the activities. I really enjoyed being around people with the same values, interests, standards, and goals. It was during this same time period that I began attending institute [of religion]. It all seemed very natural: Thursday nights [5:30]—missionary discussion, followed by institute.

I learned a lot in institute and especially enjoyed our class about how to achieve a celestial marriage. The first semester ended in May, shortly after I began attending, and I felt cheated. But I was fortunate enough to catch the second semester class, Teachings of the Living Prophets. While in institute, I bought myself the four standard works and I continued to learn and grow in the Church line upon line, precept upon precept, here a little and there a little. I was baptized September 17, 1999, by another friend I had made while attending institute.

I am thankful for the institute program. It has not only shaped me, but it has also helped me qualify to become a missionary, which mission I started preparing for five months after my baptism. I have been blessed with many opportunities to serve and to teach prior to my mission.

I am thankful for my friend. I hope he realizes what he has done for me. We have both served missions, I to South Africa Durban, he to South Africa Cape Town. All it takes is a friend to bring such a mighty change in one's life. (From personal correspondence.)

Now, there seems to be nothing miraculous in that story. But there is a miracle of wisdom beyond human capacity.

Perhaps because Mbuti had walked the path himself or perhaps by revelation, he knew what his friend would have to do to endure. And so he knew how to lift and help.

He introduced his friend to the missionaries. He saw that

his friend was baptized and received the gift of the Holy Ghost. He took his friend, even before baptism, to where he would study the scriptures and thus be nurtured by the good word of God. Even before baptism he helped his friend discover this promise: "Wherefore, I said unto you, feast upon the words of Christ; for behold, the words of Christ will tell you all things what ye should do" (2 Nephi 32:3). The words must have told him to buy scriptures, which he did.

At baptism, Brother Lupahla received the gift of the Holy Ghost to serve as his constant companion as long as he invited it and lived worthy of it. That assured him of another promise, "For behold, again I say unto you that if ye will enter in by the way, and receive the Holy Ghost, it will show unto you all things what ye should do" (2 Nephi 32:5). The Holy Ghost must have told him to begin to prepare for a mission, which he did.

We do not know which friends went with him to his sacrament meetings both before and after baptism, but some must have greeted him warmly, as they did on his first visit. There, he renewed his covenant to always remember the Savior, to keep His commandments, and to receive again the promise of the companionship of the Holy Ghost. We don't know what part his friends had in his calls to serve and to speak. But we can be sure that they thanked him and told him when they felt the Spirit in his service and in his teaching.

We can know something of his private life. Remember that he wrote that he continued to learn. He wrote that he grew "in the Church line upon line, precept upon precept, here a little and there a little." He said that he had been shaped by his experiences in the Church Educational System institute. We know from the scriptures what caused those changes in him. He had to be praying with faith in the Savior. He was receiving testimony and directions through the Spirit. And then he was not only doing what he was inspired to do but he was asking God to let the Atonement work in his life.

Nephi, describing that miracle of change and what brings it, said this:

> And now, my beloved brethren, I perceive that ye ponder still in your hearts; and it grieveth me that I must speak concerning this thing. For if ye would hearken unto the Spirit which teacheth a man to pray ye would know that ye must pray; for the evil spirit teacheth not a man to pray, but teacheth him that he must not pray.
>
> But behold, I say unto you that ye must pray always, and not faint; that ye must not perform any thing unto the Lord save in the first place ye shall pray unto the Father in the name of Christ, that he will consecrate thy performance unto thee, that thy performance may be for the welfare of thy soul. (2 Nephi 32:8–9.)

The Holy Ghost is a comforter and a guide. But He is also a cleansing agent. That is why service in the kingdom is so crucial to enduring. When we are called to serve, we can pray for the Holy Ghost to be our companion with assurance He will come. When we ask in faith, a change can come in our natures both for the welfare of our souls and to strengthen us for the tests we all must face.

There are limits on what friends can do to help the ones who must endure. It is the new members who must pray. It is they who must rely on the strength they will receive in answers to their prayers. They must choose for themselves in faith to be baptized, trusting in their perfect friend, the Savior. They must choose in faith in Him to repent, to be humble and contrite.

They must choose to receive the gift of the Holy Ghost. The words of confirmation into the Church are an invitation: "Receive the Holy Ghost." And that choice must be made not once, but every day, every hour, every minute. Even when the Holy Ghost comes and inspires them what they should do, doing it or not is a choice. Even when they read the scriptures regularly, it takes a choice to "feast upon the words of Christ." And even the feast is not nourishing without a choice to do what the words of Christ tell them to do. With faith and obedience practiced long enough, the Holy Ghost becomes a constant companion, our natures change, and endurance becomes certain.

The member must make the choices, but the true friend is vital. There are important ways for us to share the new member's burden that it may be bearable. We can love, listen, show, and testify.

First, we must love them. That is what the Savior does. We can do it with Him and for Him. He showed us the way in His mortal ministry. He taught by precept and example that we are to love His disciples.

"This is my commandment, That ye love one another, as I have loved you.

"Greater love hath no man than this, that a man lay down his life for his friends.

"Ye are my friends, if ye do whatsoever I command you.

"Henceforth I call you not servants; for the servant knoweth not what his lord doeth: but I have called you friends; for all things that I have heard of my Father I have made known unto you" (John 15:12–15).

The Savior watches over the struggling member as a friend. He laid down His life for all of us. He loves us and will grant us, if we are faithful, the gift of feeling a part of His love for them. I have at times been blessed by the Holy Ghost to sense the Savior's love for a struggling new member. I know for myself that is possible.

Second, we must listen to the new member with understanding and empathy. That also will take spiritual gifts, since our experience will rarely parallel theirs. It will not be enough to say "I understand how you feel" unless we do. But the Savior does. He is prepared to help you be a friend who understands even those you have just met, if you ask in faith. Before He was born, prophets knew what He would do to be able to help you be a friend for Him:

> And he shall go forth, suffering pains and afflictions and temptations of every kind; and this that the word might be fulfilled which saith he will take upon him the pains and the sicknesses of his people.
>
> And he will take upon him death, that he may loose the bands of death which bind his people; and he will take upon him their infirmities, that his bowels may be filled with mercy, according to the flesh, that he may know according to the flesh how to succor his people according to their infirmities. (Alma 7:11–12.)

Third, we must be an example for the new member. We can feast upon the word of God. We can ask for and live for the companionship of the Holy Ghost. We can be obedient out of our faith in Jesus Christ. And in time we can become an example of a disciple who is born again through the

Atonement. It may be gradual. It may be hard for us to discern in ourselves. But it will be real. And it will give hope to the new member and to all those we befriend on the path to eternal life.

Fourth, we must testify of the truth to the new member. It must be sincere, and it is best when it is simple. It is most helpful when it is about the reality and mission of the Savior, about our Heavenly Father's love, and of the gifts and companionship of the Holy Ghost. And it is essential to testify that the Father and the Son appeared to the young Joseph Smith and that the full gospel and the true Church have been restored by heavenly messengers. The Holy Ghost will confirm those simple declarations as truth.

The new member will need that confirmation, again and again, even when we are not there to testify. Should they choose to reject the companionship of the Holy Ghost, they will not endure. But that is true for all of us, wherever we are and however faithful we have been. All of us will be tested. And all of us need true friends to love us, to listen to us, to show us the way, and to testify of truth to us so that we may retain the companionship of the Holy Ghost. You must be such a true friend.

I can still remember, as if it were today, friends who touched my life for good long ago. They are gone, but the memory of their love, example, faith, and testimony still lifts me. And your friendship to even one new member may, in this life and in the next, cause hundreds or even thousands of their ancestors and their descendants to call you blessed.

This is the true Church of Jesus Christ. He lives. He loves you, and He loves those whom you must serve and who will become your true friends forever.

— 14 —

"WRITE UPON MY HEART"

Parents should teach their children to pray. The child learns from both what the parents do and what they say. The child who sees a mother or a father pass through the trials of life with fervent prayer to God and then hears a sincere testimony that God answered in kindness will remember what they saw and heard. When their trials come, they will be prepared.

In time, when the child is away from home and family, prayer can provide the shield of protection the parent will want so much for them to have. Parting can be hard, particularly when the parent and the child know that they may not see each other for a long time. I had that experience with my father. We parted on a street corner in New York City. He had come there for his work. I was there on my way to another place. We both knew that I probably would never return to live with my parents under the same roof again.

It was a sunny day, around noontime, the streets crowded with cars and pedestrians. On that particular corner there was a traffic light which stopped the cars and the people in

From a talk given at general conference, 8 October 2000.

all directions for a few minutes. The light changed to red; the cars stopped. The crowd of pedestrians hurried off the curbs, moving every way, including diagonally, across the intersection.

The time had come for parting, and I started across the street. I stopped almost in the center, with people rushing by me. I turned to look back. Instead of moving off in the crowd, my father was still standing on the corner looking at me. To me he seemed lonely and perhaps a little sad. I wanted to go back to him, but I realized the light would change and so I turned and hurried on.

Years later I talked to him about that moment. He told me that I had misread his face. He said he was not sad; he was concerned. He had seen me look back, as if I were a little boy, uncertain and looking for assurance. He told me in those later years that the thought in his mind had been: *Will he be all right? Have I taught him enough? Is he prepared for whatever may lie ahead?*

There were more than thoughts in his mind. I knew from having watched him that he had feelings in his heart. He yearned for me to be protected, to be safe. I had heard and felt that yearning in his prayers, and even more in the prayers of my mother, for all the years I had lived with them. I had learned from that, and I remembered.

Prayer is a matter of the heart. I had been taught far more than the rules of prayer. I had learned from my parents and from the Savior's teachings that we must address our Heavenly Father in the reverent language of prayer. "Our Father . . . in heaven, hallowed be thy name" (Matthew 6:9). I knew that we never profane His sacred name—never. Can you imagine how the prayers of a child are harmed by hearing a parent profane the name of God? There will be terrible consequences for such an offense to the little ones.

I had learned that it was important to give thanks for blessings and to ask for forgiveness. "And forgive us our debts, as we forgive our debtors" (Matthew 6:12). I had been taught that we ask for what we need and pray for others to be blessed. "Give us this day our daily bread" (Matthew 6:11). I knew that we must surrender our will. "Thy kingdom come. Thy will be done in earth, as it is in heaven" (Matthew 6:10). I had been taught and found it true that we can be warned of danger and shown early what we have done that displeased God. "And lead us not into temptation, but deliver us from evil" (Matthew 6:13).

I had learned that we must always pray in the name of Jesus Christ. But something I had seen and heard had taught me those words were more than a formality. There was a picture of the Savior on the bedroom wall where my mother was bedridden in the years before she died. She had put it there because of something her cousin Samuel O. Bennion had told her. He had traveled with an Apostle who described seeing the Savior in a vision. Elder Bennion gave her that print, saying that it was the best portrayal he had ever seen of the Master's strength of character. So she framed it and placed it on the wall where she could see it from her bed.

She knew the Savior, and she loved Him. I had learned from her that we do not close in the name of a stranger when we approach our Father in prayer. I knew from what I had seen of her life that her heart was drawn to the Savior from years of determined and consistent effort to serve Him and to please Him. I knew the scripture was true that warns, "For how knoweth a man the master whom he has not served, and who is a stranger unto him, and is far from the thoughts and intents of his heart?" (Mosiah 5:13).

Years after my mother and father are gone, the words "in the name of Jesus Christ" are not casual for me, either when I say them or when I hear others say them. We must serve Him to know the Master's heart. But we also must pray that Heavenly Father will answer our prayers in our hearts as well as in our minds (see Jeremiah 31:33; 2 Corinthians 3:3; Hebrews 8:10; 10:16).

President George Q. Cannon described the blessing of people coming together having prayed for such answers. He was speaking of going to a priesthood meeting, yet many of you have gone to meetings with hearts prepared in the way he described in these words:

> I should enter that assembly with my mind entirely free from all influence that would prevent the operation of the Spirit of God upon me. I should go in a prayerful spirit, asking God to *write upon my heart* His will, not with my own will already prepared and determined to carry out my will regardless of everyone else's views. If I were to go and all the rest were to go with this spirit, then the Spirit of God would be felt in our midst, and that which we would decide upon would be the mind and will of God because God would reveal it to us. We would see light in the direction where we should go, and we would behold darkness in the direction we should not go. (George Q. Cannon, *Gospel Truth: Discourses and Writings of George Q. Cannon*, sel. Jerreld L. Newquist [Salt Lake City: Deseret Book Co., 1957], 259.)

Our goal when we teach our children to pray is for them to want God to write upon their hearts and be willing then to go and do what God asks of them. It is possible for our children to have faith enough, from what they see us do and what we teach, that they can feel at least part of what the Savior felt as He prayed to have the strength to make His infinite sacrifice for us: "And he went a little further, and fell on his face, and prayed, saying, O my Father, if it be possible, let this cup pass from me: nevertheless not as I will, but as thou wilt" (Matthew 26:39).

I have had prayers answered. Those answers were most clear when what I wanted was silenced by an overpowering need to know what God wanted. It is then that the answer from a loving Heavenly Father can be spoken to the mind by the still, small voice and can be written on the heart.

Some parents are listening with this question: "But how can I soften the heart of my child now grown older and convinced he or she doesn't need God? How can I soften a heart enough to allow God to write His will upon it?" Sometimes tragedy will soften a heart. But for some, even tragedy is not enough.

But there is one need even the hardened and proud person cannot believe they can meet for themselves. They cannot lift the weight of sin from their own shoulders. And even the most hardened may at times feel the prick of conscience and thus the need for forgiveness from God. A loving father, Alma, taught that need to his son Corianton this way: "And now, the plan of mercy could not be brought about except an atonement should be made; therefore God himself atoneth for the sins of the world, to bring about the plan of mercy, to appease the demands of justice, that God might be a perfect, just God, and a merciful God also" (Alma 42:15).

And then, after bearing testimony of the Savior and His Atonement, the father made this plea for a softened heart: "O my son, I desire that ye should deny the justice of God no more. Do not endeavor to excuse yourself in the least point because of your sins, by denying the justice of God; but do you let the justice of God, and his mercy, and his long-suffering have full sway in your heart; and let it bring you down to the dust in humility" (Alma 42:30).

Alma knew what we can know: that testifying of Jesus Christ and Him crucified had the greatest possibility of his son coming to sense his need for the help only God could give. And prayers are answered to those whose hearts are softened by that overwhelming feeling of the need for cleansing.

When we teach those we love that we are spirit children temporarily away from a loving Heavenly Father, we open the door of prayer to them.

We lived in His presence before we came here to be tested. We knew His face, and He knew ours. Just as my earthly father watched me go away from him, our Father in Heaven watched us go into mortality.

His Beloved Son, Jehovah, left those glorious courts to come down into the world to suffer what we would suffer and to pay the price of all the sins we would commit. He provided for us the only way to go home again to our Heavenly Father and to Him. If the Holy Ghost can tell us just that much about who we are, we and our children might feel what Enos felt. He prayed this way:

"And my soul hungered; and I kneeled down before my Maker, and I cried unto him in mighty prayer and supplication for mine own soul; and all the day long did I cry unto him; yea, and when the night came I did still raise my voice high that it reached the heavens.

"And there came a voice unto me, saying: Enos, thy sins are forgiven thee, and thou shalt be blessed" (Enos 1:4–5).

I can promise you that no joy will exceed what you would feel if a child of yours prays in the hour of need and receives such an answer. You will someday be separated from them, with a longing in your heart to be reunited. A loving Heavenly Father knows that longing would last forever unless we are reunited as families with Him and His Beloved Son. He put in place all His children will need to have that blessing. To find it, they must ask of God for themselves, nothing doubting, as the boy Joseph Smith did.

My dad was concerned that day in New York because he knew, as my mother knew, that the only real tragedy would be if we were apart forever. That is why they taught me to pray. They knew we could be together forever only with God's help and with His assurances. As you will do, they taught prayer best by example.

The afternoon my mother died, we went to the family home from the hospital. We sat quietly in the darkened living room for a while. Dad excused himself and went to his bedroom. He was gone for a few minutes. When he walked back into the living room, there was a smile on his face. He said that he'd been concerned for Mother. During the time he had gathered her things from her hospital room and thanked the staff for being so kind to her, he thought of her going into the spirit world just minutes after her death. He was afraid she would be lonely if there was no one to meet her.

He had gone to his bedroom to ask his Heavenly Father to have someone greet Mildred, his wife and my mother. He said that he had been told in answer to his prayer that his mother had met his sweetheart. I smiled at that too. Grandma Eyring was not very tall. I had a clear picture of her rushing through the crowd, her short legs moving rapidly on her mission to meet my mother.

Dad surely didn't intend at that moment to teach me about prayer, but he did. I can't remember a sermon from my mother or my father about prayer. They prayed when times were hard and when they were good. And they reported in matter-of-fact ways how kind God was, how powerful and how close. The prayers I heard most were about what it would take for us to be together forever. And the answers which will remain written on my heart seem most often to be the assurances that we were on the path.

When I saw in my mind my grandmother rushing to my mother, I felt joy for them and a longing to bring my sweetheart and our children to such a reunion. That longing is why we must teach our children to pray.

I testify that our Heavenly Father answers the pleadings of faithful parents to know how to teach their children to pray. I testify that because of the Atonement of Jesus Christ, we can have eternal life in families if we honor the covenants offered in this, His true Church.

— 15 —

LEADING OUR
FAMILIES TO CHRIST

Oftentimes children teach us great lessons. I realized
that again as I was reading my daily journal. The
entry for January 28, 1972, concerns my two-year-
old son and reads in part:

> Matthew supplied me a lesson. He cried, I thought
> without reason, in bed tonight. He asked several times if
> I'd blow his nose for him or hold the tissue while he blew
> his nose. After three or four trips, I stalked into his room
> and asked, "Do you want me to spank you?" He nodded
> yes. I asked again, this time illustrating with my raised
> hand. He said, "Yes." Suddenly, my heart melted as I real-
> ized he trusted me so much that if I thought a spanking
> would help his problem, that's what he wanted. I rocked
> him for a while and then realized to my further softening
> that he had a stuffed nose from a cold that was just begin-
> ning. That had been his discomfort. I got some tissues for
> him, gave them to him in bed, and told him to blow as
> much as he would like. He said, "Thanks." I went away a
> chastened man.

Here was a two-year-old giving anew an example of King

From Ensign, April 1973, 29–32.

Benjamin's discourse: "For the natural man is an enemy to God, and has been from the fall of Adam, and will be, forever and ever, unless he yields to the enticings of the Holy Spirit, and putteth off the natural man and becometh a saint through the atonement of Christ the Lord, and becometh as a child, submissive, meek, humble, patient, full of love, willing to submit to all things which the Lord seeth fit to inflict upon him, even as a child doth submit to his father" (Mosiah 3:19).

Clearly, Matthew and other children start out as King Benjamin says they must finish: submissive. But we make the mistake, too often, of putting our efforts and concerns as parents into keeping them submissive to us and to our leadership. We forget that King Benjamin phrased the problem for us differently: how do we transfer that natural submissiveness of our children to the Lord Jesus Christ? How do we help our children follow the Savior in submissiveness?

We can have far more hope of success in leading our families if we see the problem as helping them to fall in line behind us, in a line led by the Savior.

Why does the once-submissive child stop following? Because he or she loses faith. If the child could see the Master moving at the head of the line or had assurance He was there, it would be sensible to keep following, for the path would surely lead to happiness. Followership is an act of faith, and ceasing to follow is an act proclaiming loss of faith.

An older Matthew is going to look quizzically at me someday when I say, "Even though all your friends are dressing that way, it's better that you don't." Oh, what a test of faith that will be for him! Will he choose to change clothes then, as he chose the spanking? That depends on some things I can't control but a few I can. We can't control completely the child nor all that happens to him. But we can direct our own behavior in three ways that will build faith for followership.

First, we can introduce our children to the Savior through prayer and the scriptures. They can't, with their physical eyes, see Him leading their family, but they can feel His reality. That means we must do more than teach the mechanics of prayer and more than simply make the scriptures available.

One purpose of family and private prayer must be to seek spiritual experiences for our children. The nightly prayers by the bedside and the family prayers night and morning meant little for my son Henry until the day he was lost, a six-year-old trying to find home through six miles of strange country. He was running, crying, when in desperation he dashed toward a clump of bushes to pray. As he said afterwards, with wonder in his voice, "Before I even started to pray, two people walked up and asked if they could help." He was home an hour later.

It is even possible for a parent to gain spiritual experiences for a child who is no longer submissive. Remember the angel who appeared to the rebellious Alma the Younger and said: "Behold, the Lord hath heard the prayers of his people, and also the prayers of his servant, Alma, who is thy father; for he has prayed with much faith concerning thee that thou mightest be brought to the knowledge of the truth; therefore, for this purpose have I come to convince thee of the power and authority of God, that the prayers of his servants might be answered according to their faith" (Mosiah 27:14).

We can also share scripture reading with our children in a

way that makes it likely they feel spiritual assurances and can feel our acquaintance with the scriptures and the Master. President Marion G. Romney, in an address at Brigham Young University, recounted his experience reading the Book of Mormon with his son.

President Romney said: "We were each reading aloud alternate paragraphs of those last three marvelous chapters of Second Nephi. I heard his voice break and thought he had a cold, but we went on to the end of the three chapters.

"As we finished, he said to me, 'Daddy, do you ever cry when you read the Book of Mormon?'

"'Yes, son,' I answered. 'Sometimes the Spirit of the Lord so witnesses to my soul that the Book of Mormon is true that I do cry.'

"'Well,' he said, 'that is what happened to me tonight.'"

That can happen with our children if we arrange to be alone with them, if we stay with them for the time it would take to read three chapters, and if we can say honestly, "Yes, son, I do cry, too."

A second part of our children's world we can control is the happiness and joy they see us exhibit in the Lord's service. That matters to the young person deciding whether to submit. Is the Master's burden really light? Is the service joyful? Those questions will be answered for our children in our faces, voices, and actions, probably late on a long, long Sabbath day or in other times of stress, or tragedy.

I never heard my father preach about the "peace that passeth understanding," but I sensed it in his smile as we went to every church meeting together. If he frowned, it was that I was slow getting ready, not that we were going. I suppose I never considered not going, because I never saw it done. And I saw the peace in his face as we left a hospital an hour after my mother died. He left me and walked back into the hospital ward to thank the nurses and doctors, more concerned for them than for himself. He didn't say so, but I knew the burden was light only because he trusted the Master. Much as Matthew trusted me.

Elder Mark E. Petersen's questions suggest the paradox of trying to urge children to a service we do not rejoice in ourselves:

> If the parents do not know the thrill of a clear conscience, can they teach its joy to their little ones?
>
> If parents have never known the satisfaction which comes through the payment of an honest tithe, can they plant the seeds of obedience to this law in the hearts of their children?
>
> If parents have never discovered the true value of keeping holy the Sabbath Day, can they teach their children to honor it?
>
> If parents have never caught the vision of the clean life, can they picture it to the members of their families?
>
> If parents have never been in the temple, can they teach their children the great advantages of temple marriage?
>
> If father and mother have given no thought to the meaning of a mission, can they develop in the hearts of their sons and daughters a desire to perform one?
>
> If parents themselves are not fully converted to the Gospel, can they effectively convert their own children? (*A Faith to Live By* [Salt Lake City: Bookcraft, 1959], 112–13.)

A third experience we can control is giving assignments

to our children that will build their faith that Christ does lead human beings who submit to him. With that faith, it will be far easier to believe that dad could be right when he gives an apparently unreasonable direction, after seeking divine help. Father Lehi set the great example for us in his training of Nephi. Nephi says in the first chapter of the Book of Mormon that he was "born of goodly parents, therefore I was taught somewhat in all the learning of my father" (1 Nephi 1:1). But Father Lehi did far more than that. He gave Nephi the chance to know that God guides submissive men and women, in detail and in the midst of danger and difficulty. Lehi sent his sons back to Jerusalem for the plates of Laban. Only Nephi gained the great advantage from that dangerous mission of learning for himself that the Master leads. He said:

"And it was by night; and I caused that they [his brothers] should hide themselves without the walls. And after they had hid themselves, I, Nephi, crept into the city and went forth towards the house of Laban.

"And I was led by the Spirit, not knowing beforehand the things which I should do" (1 Nephi 4:5–6).

He got the plates and returned safely with his brothers to their father and mother. Beyond the great blessing of the plates as scripture for his posterity, Lehi gained an invaluable experience for his son Nephi. Nephi would have faith in following a "visionary man," for he knew that the Master really leads.

We see the fruits of that experience coming back to bless Lehi in the leadership of his family. As they struggled in the wilderness, he had great difficulty in maintaining the faith of his children in his leadership. At one low point Nephi had broken his bow, and the fear of starvation raised again the feelings of rebellion in some of Lehi's family. Nephi made a bow with his own hands; then, instead of simply going out to hunt for food, he turned to his father and said, "Whither shall I go to obtain food?" Then Nephi records, "And it came to pass that he did inquire of the Lord . . ." (1 Nephi 16:23–24).

Nephi was submissive to his father, at least partly because of experiences that had assured him that God does answer prayers even in minute concerns of men and families. Lehi had wisely provided experiences where Nephi could find that out for himself. A child can be given responsibilities in settings that make it likely he will turn to God for guidance. With those experiences, he can far more easily feel confident and safe in following a father who also seeks this help.

One father, after seeking the help of the Lord, gathered his family together before deciding to accept a job in another city. He asked the family their advice on the desirability of the move and gave them the opportunity to go to the Lord and receive an answer for themselves as to what they should do. After they had prayed, they felt inspired, as the father did, that they should make the move. Thus, because he gave them the opportunity to get the spiritual answer that he had also received, they were able to believe and follow his counsel.

As difficult as it is to make it possible for our children to follow us, it may be at least as hard to help our wives follow our lead. Many of us have wives of great abilities, great faith, and great forcefulness, and yet, in the Doctrine and Covenants the Lord seems to suggest that both the Prophet's wife, Emma, and our own wives should be submissive. He says, "Continue in the spirit of meekness, and beware of pride. Let thy soul delight in thy husband, and the glory which shall come upon him" (D&C 25:14).

How can a strong woman accept that? The Doctrine and Covenants seems to be answering that question specifically: "No power or influence can or ought to be maintained by virtue of the priesthood, only by persuasion, by long-suffering, by gentleness and meekness, and by love unfeigned; by kindness, and pure knowledge, which shall greatly enlarge the soul without hypocrisy, and without guile" (D&C 121: 41–42).

It would be hard to find a better marriage manual. Certainly the ablest, the most faithful, and the most forceful woman could feel confident in following a leader who, with love unfeigned, uses persuasion, kindness, and long-suffering.

And again, we are told that if we exercise our priesthood righteously, ". . . then shall thy confidence wax strong in the presence of God; and the doctrine of the priesthood shall distil upon thy soul as the dews from heaven.

"The Holy Ghost shall be thy constant companion, and thy scepter an unchanging scepter of righteousness and truth; and thy dominion shall be an everlasting dominion, and without compulsory means it shall flow unto thee forever and ever" (D&C 121:45–46).

Winning the faith of children and wives will require not only a change of heart for many of us, but also the courage to endure. Even great fathers sometimes lose the faith of some of their families. Father Lehi endured through that disappointment. He even had warnings that this disappointment would come. In a dream he beckoned his family to follow him to the sweet fruit of the gospel, but Laman and Lemuel would not. For most of us, such a dream would be enough to embitter us and stop us from trying to lead. That is not the way Lehi reacted. At the end of his life Lehi was still teaching all of his family, urging them to follow Jesus Christ. In what he must have known were nearly his last words to his family, he said, "Awake, my sons; put on the armor of righteousness. Shake off the chains with which ye are bound, and come forth out of obscurity, and arise from the dust" (2 Nephi 1:23).

The hope of the father that his sons would follow might seem tragic if you look only at the few years of Lehi's life and Laman and Lemuel's rebellion. But his hope must now seem realized in the great blessings poured out upon his seed, the Lamanites in our day. By enduring, by never stopping his beckoning to follow the Savior, Lehi still reaches out to his family today. And thousands embrace the gospel and raise righteous posterity—Lehi's posterity.

We cannot assure perfect obedience of all our children, but we can nurture faith in our families that Christ lives, that His service is joyful, and that He speaks to those who would follow Him. The submissive child will hear His voice and follow us as we follow the Master.

Blessing
Others
in Love

— 16 —

"Watch with Me"

Whether the brethren of the Church accepted the priesthood, we took upon us the responsibility to do our part in watching over the Church. None of us can escape accountability. The president of the priesthood in all the earth bears the total responsibility. Through the keys of the priesthood, each quorum bears its part. Even the newest deacon in the most distant place on earth has a part in the great responsibility to watch over the Church.

Consider these words from the Doctrine and Covenants: "Therefore, let every man stand in his own office, and labor in his own calling; and let not the head say unto the feet it hath no need of the feet; for without the feet how shall the body be able to stand?" And then the Savior includes even the deacons in His listing of assignments: "The deacons and teachers should be appointed to watch over the church, to be standing ministers unto the church" (D&C 84:109, 111).

I pray that I might explain our sacred trust so that even the newest deacon and the convert most recently ordained

From a talk given at general conference, 31 March 2001.

will see his opportunity. In many places in the scriptures, the Lord has described Himself and those He calls to the priesthood as shepherds. A shepherd watches over sheep. In the scriptural stories, the sheep are in danger; they need protection and nourishment. The Savior warns us that we must watch the sheep as He does. He gave His life for them. They are His. We cannot approach His standard if, like a hired servant, we watch only when it is convenient and only for a reward. Here is His standard:

"I am the good shepherd: the good shepherd giveth his life for the sheep.

"But he that is an hireling, and not the shepherd, whose own the sheep are not, seeth the wolf coming, and leaveth the sheep, and fleeth: and the wolf catcheth them, and scattereth the sheep" (John 10:11–12).

The members of the Church are the sheep. They are His, and we are called by Him to watch over them. We are to do more than warn them against danger. We are to feed them. Once, long ago, the Lord commanded His prophet to rebuke the shepherds of Israel. Here is the warning, which is still in force, in the words of the prophet Ezekiel: "And the word of the Lord came unto me, saying, Son of man, prophesy against the shepherds of Israel, . . . and say unto them, Thus saith the Lord God unto the shepherds; Woe be to the shepherds of Israel that do feed themselves! should not the shepherds feed the flocks?" (Ezekiel 34:1–2).

The food those shepherds took for themselves, letting the sheep starve, could lead to salvation for the sheep. One of the great shepherds in the Book of Mormon described both what that food is and how it can be provided: "And after they had been received unto baptism, and were wrought upon and cleansed by the power of the Holy Ghost, they were numbered among the people of the church of Christ; and their names were taken, that they might be remembered and nourished by the good word of God, to keep them in the right way, to keep them continually watchful unto prayer, relying alone upon the merits of Christ, who was the author and the finisher of their faith" (Moroni 6:4).

It is painful to imagine a shepherd feeding himself and letting the sheep go hungry. Yet I have seen many shepherds who feed their flocks. One was the president of a deacons quorum. One of his quorum members lived near my home. That neighbor boy had never attended a quorum meeting or done anything with the members of his quorum. His stepfather was not a member, and his mother did not attend church.

The presidency of his deacons quorum met in council one Sunday morning. Each week they were fed the good word of God by the fine adviser and teacher. In their presidency meeting, those thirteen-year-old shepherds remembered the boy who never came. They talked about how much he needed what they received. The president assigned his counselor to go after that wandering sheep.

I knew the counselor, and I knew he was shy, and I knew the difficulty of the assignment, so I watched with wonder through my front window as the counselor trudged by my house, going up the road to the home of the boy who never came to church. The shepherd had his hands in his pockets. His eyes were on the ground. He walked slowly, the way you would if you weren't sure you wanted to get where you were headed. In twenty minutes or so, he came back down the road with the lost deacon walking by his side. That scene was repeated for a few more Sundays. Then the boy who had been lost and was found moved away.

Now, that story seems unremarkable. It was just three boys sitting in a room around a small table. Then it was a boy walking up a road and coming back with another boy. But years later, I was in a stake conference, a continent away from the room in which that presidency had met in council. A gray-haired man came up to me and said quietly, "My grandson lived in your ward years ago." With tenderness, he told me of that boy's life. And then he asked if I could find that deacon who walked slowly up that road. And he wondered if I could thank him and tell him that his grandson, now grown to be a man, still remembered.

He remembered because in those few weeks he had been, for the first time in his life that he recognized, watched over by the shepherds of Israel. He had been warned by hearing eternal truth from people who cared about him. He had been offered the bread of life. And young shepherds had been true to their trust from the Lord.

It is not easy to learn to do that well and do it consistently. The Savior showed us how, and how to train others to do it. He established His Church. He had to leave His Church in the hands of inexperienced servants, just as many of us are. He knew they would face difficulties beyond their human powers to resolve. What He did for them can be a guide for us.

When the Savior went to the Garden of Gethsemane to suffer bitter agonies before His betrayal and sufferings on the cross, He could have gone alone. But He took His priesthood servants with Him. Here is the account from Matthew: "Then saith he unto them, My soul is exceeding sorrowful, even unto death: tarry ye here, and *watch with me*" (Matthew 26:38; emphasis added).

The Savior prayed to His Father for strength. In the midst of His agony, He returned to Peter to teach him what it requires for all who would watch with Him: "And he cometh unto the disciples, and findeth them asleep, and saith unto Peter, What, could ye not watch with me one hour? Watch and pray, that ye enter not into temptation: the spirit indeed is willing, but the flesh is weak" (Matthew 26:40–41).

There is a reassurance and a warning in that simple exchange of the Master with His shepherds. He watches with us. He who sees all things, whose love is endless, and who never sleeps—He watches with us. He knows what the sheep need at every moment. By the power of the Holy Ghost, He can tell us and send us to them. And we can by the priesthood invite His power to bless them.

But His warning to Peter is to us as well. The wolf who would kill the sheep will surely tear at the shepherd. So we must watch over ourselves as well as others. As a shepherd, we will be tempted to go near the edges of sin. But sin in any form offends the Holy Ghost. You must not do anything or go anywhere that offends the Spirit. You cannot afford that risk. Should sin cause you to fail, you would be responsible not only for your own sins but for the sorrow you might have prevented in the lives of others had you been worthy to hear and obey the whisperings of the Spirit. The shepherd must be able to hear the voice of the Spirit and bring down the powers of heaven or he will fail.

The warning given to an ancient prophet is a warning to us as well:

"So thou, O son of man, I have set thee a watchman unto the house of Israel; therefore thou shalt hear the word at my mouth, and warn them from me.

"When I say unto the wicked, O wicked man, thou shalt surely die; if thou dost not speak to warn the wicked from his way, that wicked man shall die in his iniquity; but his blood will I require at thine hand" (Ezekiel 33:7–8).

The penalty for failure is great. But the Lord taught Peter how to build the foundation for success. He repeated a simple message three times. It was that love for the Lord would be in the heart of a true shepherd. Here is the end of the account: "He saith unto him the third time, Simon, son of Jonas, lovest thou me? Peter was grieved because he said unto him the third time, Lovest thou me? And he said unto him, Lord, thou knowest all things; thou knowest that I love thee. Jesus saith unto him, Feed my sheep" (John 21:17).

It is love that must motivate the shepherds of Israel. That may seem difficult at the start, because we may not even know the Lord well. But if we begin with even a little grain of faith in Him, our service to the sheep will increase our love for Him and for them. It comes from simple things that every shepherd must do. We pray for the sheep, every one for whom we are responsible. When we ask, "Please tell me who needs me," answers will come. A face or a name will come into our minds. Or we may have a chance meeting that we feel isn't chance. In those moments, we will feel the love of the Savior for them and for us. As you watch over His sheep, your love for Him will grow. And that will increase your confidence and your courage.

Now, you may be thinking: *It's not that easy for me. I have so many people to watch over. And I have so little time.* But where the Lord calls He prepares a way, His way. There are shepherds who believe that. I'll tell you about one.

Two years ago, a man was called as the president of his elders quorum. He had been a member of the Church for less than ten years. He had just become worthy to be sealed to his wife and family in the temple. His wife was an invalid. He had three daughters. The oldest was thirteen, and she cooked the meals and, with the others, cared for the house. His scant earnings from manual labor supported not only those five people but a grandfather who lived with them in their small house.

When he was called to be president of his elders quorum, it had 13 members. That tiny quorum was responsible for another 101 men who either had no priesthood at all or who were deacons, teachers, or priests. He was responsible to watch over the souls of 114 families, with little hope that he could devote more than his Sundays and perhaps one night a week to his service, with all he did to serve his own family.

The difficulty of what he faced drove him to his knees in prayer. Then he stood up and went to work. In his efforts to meet and know his sheep, his prayers were answered in a way he had not expected. He came to see beyond individuals. He came to know that the Lord's purpose was for him to build families. And even with his limited experience, he knew that the way to build families would be to help them qualify to make and keep temple covenants.

He began to do what a good shepherd always does, but he did it differently when he saw the temple as their destination. First, he prayed to know who were to be his counselors to go with him. And then he prayed to know which families needed him and had been prepared.

He called on as many as he could. Some were cold and did not accept his friendship. But with those who did, he followed a pattern. As soon as he saw interest and trust, he invited them to meet the bishop. He had asked the bishop beforehand: "Please tell them what it takes to be worthy to go to the temple to claim its blessings for them and their families. And then please testify to them, as I have, that it will be worth it."

A few then accepted the quorum president's invitation to a temple preparation class taught by stake leaders. Not all completed the course and not all qualified for the temple. But each family and each father was prayed for. Most were invited at least once to a feast of the good word of God. With every invitation came the president's testimony of the blessings of being a family sealed forever and the sadness of being separated. Every invitation was issued with the love of the Savior.

During the president's service, he has seen twelve of the men he taught ordained elders. He has seen four of his elders ordained high priests. Those numbers don't come close to measuring the miracle. The families of those men will be blessed over generations. Fathers and mothers are now sealed to each other and to their children. They are praying over their children, receiving the help of heaven, and teaching the gospel with the love and inspiration the Lord gives to faithful parents.

That president and his counselors have become true shepherds. They have watched over the flock with the Master and have come to love Him. They are eyewitnesses to the truth of what the Savior taught an Apostle, Thomas B. Marsh. It is true for all who watch with the Lord over His sheep:

"Go your way whithersoever I will, and it shall be given you by the Comforter what you shall do and whither you shall go.

"Pray always, lest you enter into temptation and lose your reward.

"Be faithful unto the end, and lo, I am with you. These words are not of man nor of men, but of me, even Jesus Christ, your Redeemer, by the will of the Father. Amen" (D&C 31:11–13).

I testify that God the Father lives and answers our prayers. I am a witness that the loving Savior watches over His sheep with His faithful shepherds.

— 17 —

"Feed My Lambs"

The Savior taught Peter and His other Apostles and disciples why and how they were to nourish others. You remember that in the Bible account He fed them before He taught them. He had been crucified and then resurrected. His servants had gone to Galilee. They had fished through the night, catching nothing. When they drew near to shore, in the dawn, they did not at first recognize Him. He called out to them, telling them where to cast their nets, and when they did the nets were filled. They rushed to greet Him on the shore.

They found a fire of coals with fish cooking and bread. I have often wondered, as you may have done, who laid the fire, who caught the fish, and who cooked the meal, but it was the Master who prepared His disciples to be fed more than fish and bread. He let them eat first. And then He taught them of spiritual feeding. And He gave a commandment to them which still stands for each of us.

"So when they had dined, Jesus saith to Simon Peter, Simon, son of Jonas, lovest thou me more than these? He

From a talk given at general conference, 5 October 1997.

saith unto him, Yea, Lord; thou knowest that I love thee. He saith unto him, Feed my lambs" (John 21:15).

The Saints of God have always been under covenant to nourish each other spiritually, especially those tender in the gospel. We are blessed to live in a time when a great increase in that capacity to nourish new members of the Church must and therefore will be poured out upon the faithful Saints. That power has been given before among the Lord's people. This is the description of how the Lord's people did it once in a time recounted in the Book of Mormon. "They were numbered . . . that they might be remembered and nourished by the good word of God, to keep them in the right way, to keep them continually watchful unto prayer, relying alone upon the merits of Christ, who was the author and the finisher of their faith" (Moroni 6:4).

All of us have tried at some time to nourish another person's faith. Most of us have felt the concern of others for our own faith, and with it we have felt their love. More than a few of us have had a child look up to us and say, "Would you like to go to church with me?" or "Would you pray with me?" And we have had our disappointments. Someone we love may not have accepted our attempts to nourish their faith. We know from painful experience that God respects the choice of His children not to be nourished. Yet this is a time to feel renewed optimism and hope that our power to nourish will be increased.

The Lord through His living prophet has told us that He will preserve the bounteous harvest of new converts entering the waters of baptism across the earth. And the Lord will do it through us. So we can have confidence that by doing simple things, things that even a child can do, we will soon be granted greater power to nourish tender faith.

The place to start is with our own hearts. What we want with all our hearts will determine in large degree whether we can claim our right to the companionship of the Holy Ghost, without which there can be no spiritual nourishing. We can begin today to try to see those we are to nourish as our Heavenly Father sees them and so feel some of what He feels for them.

Those new members of the Church are His children. He has known them and they have known Him in the world before this one. His purpose and that of His Son, the Lord Jesus Christ, is to have them return to Him and to give them eternal life if only they will choose it. He has led and sustained His missionaries by the Holy Spirit to find and teach and baptize them. He allowed His Son to pay the price of their sins. Our Father and the Savior see those converts as tender lambs, purchased with a price we cannot fathom.

A mortal parent may appreciate, in some small way, the feelings of a loving Heavenly Father. When our children come to the age when they must leave our direct care, we feel anxiety for their safety and concern that those who are to help them will not fail them. We can feel at least some of the Father's and the Savior's love for the new members of the Church and the trust they place in us to nourish.

Those feelings in our hearts for the new members will go far to qualify us for the help of the Spirit and thus overcome the fears which may deter us from our sacred responsibility. It is wise to fear that our own skills are inadequate to meet the charge we have to nourish the faith of others. Our own abilities, however great, will not be enough. But that realistic view of our limitations creates a humility which can lead to dependence on the Spirit and thus to power.

Brigham Young told us to have courage despite our weaknesses. He did it in this language that seems so much like him:

> In addressing a congregation, though the speaker be unable to say more than half a dozen sentences, and those awkwardly constructed, if his heart is pure before God, those few broken sentences are of more value than the greatest eloquence without the Spirit of the Lord and of more real worth in the sight of God, angels, and all good men. In praying, though a person's words be few and awkwardly expressed, if the heart is pure before God, that prayer will avail more than the eloquence of a Cicero. What does the Lord, the Father of us all, care about our mode of expression? The simple, honest heart is of more avail with the Lord than all the pomp, pride, splendor, and eloquence produced by men. When he looks upon a heart full of sincerity, integrity, and child-like simplicity, he sees a principle that will endure forever—"That is the spirit of my own kingdom—the spirit I have given to my children." (*Discourses of Brigham Young,* sel. John A. Widtsoe [Salt Lake City: Deseret Book Co., 1954], 169.)

A child can do the things which will give us power to nourish the faith of others. Children could invite a recent convert to come with them to a meeting. Children could smile and greet a new member coming into a chapel or into a class. So can we. And as surely as we do, the Holy Ghost will be our companion. The fear of not knowing what to say and of being rejected will be taken from us. The newcomer will not appear to be a stranger to us. And the Holy Ghost will begin nourishing them even before we have spoken of gospel truths.

It does not require a calling more than being a member to nourish by reaching out in kindness. And even those who have no calling to teach or to preach can nourish with the good word of God if they prepare for it. We can do it every time we speak with a new member and every time we participate in a class discussion. Every word we speak can strengthen or weaken faith. We need help from the Spirit to speak the words that will nourish and strengthen.

There are two great keys to inviting the Spirit to guide what words we speak as we feed others. They are the daily study of the scriptures and the prayer of faith.

The Holy Ghost will guide what we say if we study and ponder the scriptures every day. The words of the scriptures invite the Holy Spirit. The Lord said it this way: "Seek not to declare my word, but first seek to obtain my word, and then shall your tongue be loosed; then, if you desire, you shall have my Spirit and my word, yea, the power of God unto the convincing of men" (D&C 11:21). With daily study of the scriptures, we can count on this blessing even in casual conversations or in a class when we may be asked by a teacher to respond to a question. We will experience the power the Lord promised: "Neither take ye thought beforehand what ye shall say; but treasure up in your minds continually the words of life, and it shall be given you in the very hour that portion that shall be meted unto every man" (D&C 84:85).

We treasure the word of God not only by reading the words of the scriptures but by studying them. We may be nourished more by pondering a few words, allowing the Holy

Ghost to make them treasures to us, than to pass quickly and superficially over whole chapters of scripture.

Just as pondering the scriptures invites the Holy Ghost, so does daily pleading in prayer. If we do not ask in prayer, He will rarely come, and without our petition He is not likely to linger. "And the Spirit shall be given unto you by the prayer of faith; and if ye receive not the Spirit ye shall not teach" (D&C 42:14). Heartfelt, constant pleading for the companionship of the Holy Ghost, with the pure intent to nourish our Father's children, will surely bring blessings to us and to those we love and serve.

The good word of God with which we must nourish is the simple doctrine of the gospel. We need not fear either simplicity or repetition. The Lord himself described how that doctrine goes into the hearts of men and women to nourish them:

> Behold, verily, verily, I say unto you, I will declare unto you my doctrine.
>
> And this is my doctrine, and it is the doctrine which the Father hath given unto me; and I bear record of the Father, and the Father beareth record of me, and the Holy Ghost beareth record of the Father and me; and I bear record that the Father commandeth all men, everywhere, to repent and believe in me.
>
> And whoso believeth in me, and is baptized, the same shall be saved; and they are they who shall inherit the kingdom of God.
>
> And whoso believeth not in me, and is not baptized, shall be damned.
>
> Verily, verily, I say unto you, that this is my doctrine, and I bear record of it from the Father; and whoso believeth in me believeth in the Father also; and unto him

will the Father bear record of me, for he will visit him with fire and with the Holy Ghost. (3 Nephi 11:31–35.)

The Lord went on to describe those who would be nourished by that simple doctrine and so endure, those who would inherit the celestial kingdom, as those who were childlike. It takes a childlike heart to feel the promptings of the Spirit, to surrender to those commands, and to obey. That is what it takes to be nourished by the good word of God.

And that is why we can be so optimistic in our charge to nourish the new members of the Church. However much or little they know of the doctrine, they have just submitted humbly to the ordinance of baptism and received the right to the companionship of the Holy Ghost. And so the very tenderness of their faith, which leads the Savior to refer to them as lambs, comes at a time when they have proven themselves willing to do what the Savior asks of them.

If the full requirements of their new membership are explained clearly and with love, if the opportunity to serve in the Church is extended wisely and their performance in that service judged with charity and nurtured with patient encouragement, they will be strengthened by the companionship of the Holy Ghost and then they will be nurtured by power beyond our own. As they endure, even the gates of hell will not prevail against them.

Brigham Young made the promise of how their strength to stand would grow in these words: "Those who humble themselves before the Lord, and wait upon Him with a perfect heart and willing mind, will receive little by little, line upon line, precept upon precept, here a little, and there a little, 'Now and again,' as brother John Taylor says, until they receive a certain amount. Then they have to nourish and cherish what they receive, and make it their constant companion, encouraging every good thought, doctrine and principle and doing every good work they can perform, until by and bye the Lord is in them a well of water, springing up unto everlasting life" (in *Journal of Discourses*, 4:286–87).

That is what it means in Moroni when it says, "Relying alone upon the merits of Christ, who was the author and the finisher of their faith" (Moroni 6:4). It is the Savior who made possible our being purified through His Atonement and our obedience to His commandments. And it is the Savior who will nourish those who go down in faith into the waters of baptism and receive the gift of the Holy Ghost. When they always remember Him, and when they continue in childlike obedience, it is He who will assure that they have His Spirit always to be with them.

You and I can and will by small means be part of a great work. We will study and pray and serve to qualify for the companionship of the Holy Ghost. We will then be allowed to see the new members as precious, beloved children of our Heavenly Father, and we will be led to nourish them with love, with the opportunity to serve, and with the good word of God. And then we will see in our own time what the great missionary Ammon described to his missionary companions, just as we are now companions to the missionaries laboring across the world:

> Behold, the field was ripe, and blessed are ye, for ye did thrust in the sickle, and did reap with your might, yea, all the day long did ye labor; and behold the number of

your sheaves! And they shall be gathered into the garners, that they are not wasted.

Yea, they shall not be beaten down by the storm at the last day; yea, neither shall they be harrowed up by the whirlwinds; but when the storm cometh they shall be gathered together in their place, that the storm cannot penetrate to them; yea, neither shall they be driven with fierce winds whithersoever the enemy listeth to carry them.

But behold, they are in the hands of the Lord of the harvest, and they are his; and he will raise them up at the last day. (Alma 26:5–7.)

We can by simple obedience help the Lord to take the lambs, His lambs, into His hands and take them in His arms home to their Father and our Father. I know that God will pour out the powers of heaven upon us as we join in preserving that sacred harvest of souls.

— 18 —

"Because of Your Steadiness"

From the islands of the Pacific to the highlands of South America, I've seen boys working to turn dreams into reality. In fact, I've seen it so often that it merges into one image, one picture. It's of a small boy, maybe nine or ten, in shorts, barefoot, and with a torn shirt. He's on a patch of dirt, alone, and he's looking down at a white-and-black-checkered ball. He takes a step toward it, his leg swings through, and the ball shoots off, about seven feet above the ground, where it might zip past a goalie into the net—except there's no goalie and no net; there's just the boy and the ball. And then he runs to the ball, puts it in place with his foot, and kicks it. And he does it over and over again.

You don't know where he lives, but you know that he'll take the ball home with him and that more than likely he keeps it near the place he sleeps. He sees it when he gets up and when he goes to bed. He may even dream about that ball shooting toward the goal.

You know that because you've done something like it yourself. It may have been a basketball. I can remember looking

From a talk given at general conference, 2 April 1988.

down at the ball in my hands on one freezing winter day and seeing my bloody fingerprints on the ball. I'd been outside so long that the cold had cracked the skin on my fingertips, but my mind and my eye were on the orange rim. I can still remember it, including the chipped paint on the front edge of the rim where you'd lock your eye and know the ball would fall just past that spot into the dirt-stained net. I can still remember the mark on the driveway I'd dribble to and know I was at the top of the key. I'd spin and jump for that last second shot, with the score tied. And I'd do it again and again, sometimes for hours, feeling neither time nor the cold.

You may have learned endurance playing a trumpet, or throwing a football, or riding a bucking horse, or drawing a picture. But you learned what we all did. Effort only "now and then" didn't take you far. The dreams that turned into reality stuck with you nearly all the time. You worked at them, either in fact or in your thoughts, every day and almost every hour.

It shouldn't surprise us, then, that the Lord has said to you and to me, "Watch over the church always, and be with and strengthen them" (D&C 20:53). God loves us, and He intends for us to become like Him. He doesn't ask us now to worry about all His children in all the world, as He does. Instead, He begins with a call to watch over just a few families, just a few people. But He knows that to visit thirty minutes every month with the same lesson for every family would never produce the progress He wants for us.

And so He commands, "Watch over [them] always, and be with and strengthen them." You can't be with them twenty-four hours a day. That would be "always," wouldn't it?

But they can be in your heart always. If you'll think about the families you visit, those of you who are blessed to be called home teachers, you know the help they need is beyond your casual effort.

In my experience, I've been assigned to watch over people who struggled with divorce, with financial ruin, with children who would not respond to all that parents had done, or with disease that would not respond to all that faith and medicine could do. I've gone to a home where little twin girls were sent to the screen door to tell us that Mommy and Daddy were sleeping and couldn't we come another time.

I knew in my heart that effort "now and then" wasn't enough, that "going out home teaching" or even "giving a good lesson" wouldn't do it. God called us to watch over and help people in all their struggles for physical and spiritual well-being. He called us to help by the Spirit. He called us to teach by the Spirit. He called us to live what we teach. He called us to bear testimony. He called us to love them.

Now, He didn't make it that hard just to test you. He gave you so high a calling because He loves you. He wants you home again, and to get there you have to become like Him. So He gives you a calling that can be done only with persistence and endurance.

Let's suppose you and I are companions. I know we may not have gotten together often to prepare, but let's do it tonight. Let's imagine that you and I are at my house. You've come over for a few minutes, and we're sitting at my kitchen table.

We won't talk about home teaching visits or lessons first. We'll talk about our families for a while. We'll find that some of them are struggling. And that will humble us, knowing that the Lord is counting on us. We might talk about what we know the bishop and the Relief Society and some neighbors are doing to help. And we might talk about some things we have done and could do.

Then, we'll get around to talking about one family and what we might teach them. I'll push the *Ensign* across the table to you, opened to the First Presidency message from President Hinckley. You look down and see the title, "Overpowering the Goliaths in Our Lives." That looks like the perfect lesson, doesn't it? There's only the mom and dad at home. They worry about her health problems, wondering if they're doing all they can and should. On top of that, they probably aren't sleeping much because of their son. He's still in the same town, but he's living with his friends. He won't be there when we call, but he'll be in their minds, and what he's doing and not doing will be tearing at their hearts. They'll be wondering what they can do for him. If people ever wanted and needed the Lord's help with challenges, these folks do.

Let's agree that we'll both prepare the lesson. But I think they have such respect for you that you ought to take the lead. We can't do them any good unless the Holy Ghost is with us, so I guess we'd better do more than prepare the lesson. We'd better prepare ourselves.

First, the Holy Ghost can't be with us unless we're clean. I admire the way you try to watch what you say and do, even what you think. I guess when the Lord tells us to watch over the Church, that means watching over ourselves too. Let's read this quotation from President George Q. Cannon I keep handy. And let's agree that we'll try to follow it:

Some people have an idea that because they have entered the waters of baptism and repented of their sins then that is an end of it. What a mistake! We need to have this spirit of repentance continually; we need to pray to God to show us our conduct every day. Every night before we retire to rest we should review the thoughts, words and acts of the day and then repent of everything we have done that is wrong or that has grieved the Holy Spirit. Live this way every day and endeavor to progress every day. (*Gospel Truth*, ed. Jerreld L. Newquist [Salt Lake City: Deseret Book Co., 1987], 129.)

Second, let's pray both for forgiveness and to get answers about what to do for the family. It would help if, when we go, we tell them that the Holy Ghost can guide them; it has already guided us to do something for them. If we pray and then feel that prompting and act on it, what we do may be more important than anything we say. Maybe our finding out how to help them will lead them to find out what more they can do for their son.

Let's agree that we'll include both the parents and their children in our personal prayers, and we'll plead for the Holy Ghost to help us teach. You remember the promise, "And the Spirit shall be given unto you by the prayer of faith; and if ye receive not the Spirit ye shall not teach" (D&C 42:14). That really fits us, doesn't it?

Third, we're going to be teaching a gospel principle, so we'd better study and ponder the scriptures. You remember that the Lord said, "Teach the principles of my gospel, which are in the Bible and the Book of Mormon, in the which is the fulness of the gospel" (D&C 42:12). I know you've been reading the Book of Mormon regularly. So have I. Why don't we think about our family and the gifts of the Spirit while we read? If we do, I'm sure that we'll understand and feel some things that are new to us. And we'll teach and bear testimony in their home with more power.

It won't hurt to bear testimony from our own experience that we felt the Spirit while we read the scriptures. Then they may try reading and pondering. If they do, they'll get the prompting of the Holy Ghost for themselves. And that will help them more than just feeling it when we're there.

Then we'll have a prayer together before you leave. In the next day or two we may stop by the house to do something for the family before we get there for a lesson.

The night we teach them, things will seem about as they have before, with a few exceptions. An idea and a scripture will come into your mind as you teach. You'll bear testimony of the Savior with more feeling. Perhaps we will both find our hearts drawn out to the people more. And they may linger at the door a little longer than usual as we go.

Maybe only some of that will happen. But that won't discourage us. We thought it would take repeated, steady effort. The desire of our hearts is to help others taste the fruit of the gospel. We know it won't come quickly or easily after a single effort, for them or for us. But in that visit, or in one that will come later, you will feel a warmth in your heart and truth will come into your mind. And that will bring you joy. It may go away, but you will remember it. Then you will be able to imagine what it would be like to have the Holy Ghost for your constant companion in this life and to feel the love and approval of the Savior and your Father in Heaven for eternity.

Alma knew what having that desire in our hearts and visualizing it with faith would mean to us. It would keep us going when the going was hard. Here's what he said: "And thus, if ye will not nourish the word, looking forward with an eye of faith to the fruit thereof, ye can never pluck of the fruit of the tree of life.

"But if ye will nourish the word, yea, nourish the tree as it beginneth to grow, by your faith with great diligence, and with patience, looking forward to the fruit thereof, it shall take root; and behold it shall be a tree springing up unto everlasting life" (Alma 32:40–41).

By the power of the Holy Ghost and with the eye of faith, we have glimpsed and we can look forward to the fruit of the gospel. That is the desire of our hearts. And wanting it will give us the power to keep going, with great diligence and patience.

The little boy in my memory keeps kicking that ball, over and over again. I can't see a goalpost or a goalie. I can't hear the roar of the crowd. But in his mind, he can. And so he kicks the ball, over and over again.

I pray that we will take the great opportunity God has given us to prepare ourselves. He has trusted us as watchmen of the souls of His children. He has given us a way to look forward to the fruit of the gospel by giving us a calling that requires our whole hearts. As the boy's dreams of kicking the winning goal draw him back to persistent practice with that ball, so our vision of the fruits of the gospel will draw us back to persistent repentance and prayer and study and service.

I pray that the Lord may say of us, as Alma said of his son Shiblon: "And now, my son, I trust that I shall have great joy in you, because of your steadiness and your faithfulness unto God; for as you have commenced in your youth to look to the Lord your God, even so I hope that you will continue in keeping his commandments; for blessed is he that endureth to the end" (Alma 38:2).

— 19 —

"WATCH OVER AND STRENGTHEN"

Hundreds of thousands of people in the last year were baptized and confirmed members of the Church. Each was given the opportunity of a call to serve. For them and for the Church, that experience will shape the future. Many of us remember the first time we gave a talk or conducted a meeting or knocked on the door of a home as an official visitor. My heart beats a little faster just thinking about it.

The new members may have been baptized only days or weeks before their call to serve. Some of them had never seen anyone perform the service that now was theirs. Because we have no professional clergy, the challenge of calls to serve came to more than the new members. In the last year, it is estimated that nearly two million Latter-day Saints received either a new call to be a shepherd or were given some new sheep to watch over. Just less than half of those called were youth, some as young as twelve or thirteen years of age. More than thirty thousand missionaries were called and set apart

---

From a talk given at general conference, 2 April 2000.

in that time. Most of them were less than twenty years of age. They went with only brief training and little experience.

Someone who knows organizations in the world might predict failure for a rapidly growing church depending on so many novice lay members. Even those called may well have felt some apprehension. And yet when they see through the eyes of faith the challenge as it really is, confidence replaces fear because they turn to God.

My message is first to those newly called to serve in the Church, then to those who called them, and finally to those they will serve.

First, to the newly called: Confidence depends on your seeing the call for what it is. Your call to serve is not from human beings. It is a trust from God. And the service is not simply to perform a task. Whatever name it has, every call is an opportunity and an obligation to watch over and strengthen the children of our Heavenly Father. The Savior's work is to bring to pass their immortality and eternal life (see Moses 1:39). He called us to serve others so that we could strengthen our own faith as well as theirs. He knows that by serving Him we will come to know Him.

An inspired prophet saw service as the way we come to want what the Lord wants. He wrote: "For how knoweth a man the master whom he has not served, and who is a stranger unto him, and is far from the thoughts and intents of his heart?" (Mosiah 5:13).

Because you are called by Jesus Christ to His service, you may go forward with great confidence. First, you may be assured that He knows you and your capacity to grow. He has prepared you. Calls will stretch you, often at the start and always over their course, but He will give you the Holy Ghost to be your companion. The Holy Ghost will tell you what to do when your own abilities and efforts are not enough (see John 14:26). The Holy Ghost will prompt you to bear testimony with conviction. The Savior will let you feel the love He feels for those you serve. The call is an invitation to become like Him (see 3 Nephi 27:27).

You might well ask, "How will seeing my call that way make me more confident of success?" The answer is that seeing it in that lofty way will make it more likely that you will go for help to the only source that is never-failing.

I saw a young man nearly overwhelmed by a new call not long ago. The Lord had inspired His servant to call him to be the president of a stake. The young man had never been a bishop. He had never served in a stake presidency. The stake had in it many men of greater maturity and experience.

He was humbled when he heard the call. His wife through tears said to the servant of the Lord who called him, "Are you sure?" Her husband said quietly that he would serve. His wife nodded her support, tears streaming down her face. As you might have done at such a time, he wanted to talk with his father, who was far away. He called him that afternoon on the telephone. His father has been a dairy farmer all his life. He raised the boy into a man through milking cows and letting his son observe him stop to talk with neighbors to see how they were doing. The next morning, in his first talk as a stake president, this is how he recounted the conversation with his father:

"Many of you that know me know I am a man of few words. I must have gotten that from my father. As I called him yesterday to let him know that I was being called as a stake president, his one response to me was, 'Well, you better do a lot of praying.' That was his counsel to me. What better counsel could he give?"

His father couldn't have done much better. And you can see why. The Lord is his only hope for success. Most of the help will come through the ministrations of the Holy Ghost. The Lord's servants cannot succeed without it. We can have the Holy Ghost as a companion only if we plead for it and if we qualify for it. And both require a lot of praying, praying with real faith in our Heavenly Father and in His Beloved Son and in the Holy Ghost (see D&C 90:24; Articles of Faith 1:1).

To have the companionship of the Holy Ghost, we must be cleansed of sin (see D&C 50:29). That only comes through faith enough in Jesus Christ to repent and qualify for forgiveness (see D&C 3:20). And then we have to stay away from sin. That takes prayer, both frequent and fervent (see 3 Nephi 18:18).

"You better do a lot of praying" is good counsel for all of the Lord's servants, new or seasoned. It is what His wise servants do. They pray.

The disciples of Jesus Christ when He lived on the earth noticed that about Him. He was the Son of God. He was Jehovah. And yet He prayed often enough to His Heavenly Father that His disciples realized that they must know how to pray to be His servants. So they asked Him to teach them. You remember the record:

"And it came to pass, that, as [Jesus] was praying in a

certain place, when he ceased, one of his disciples said unto him, Lord, teach us to pray, as John also taught his disciples.

"And he said unto them, When ye pray, say, Our Father which art in heaven, Hallowed be thy name. Thy kingdom come. Thy will be done, as in heaven, so in earth. . . . And forgive us our sins; for we also forgive every one that is indebted to us. And lead us not into temptation; but deliver us from evil" (Luke 11:1–2, 4; see also Matthew 6:9–13).

We seldom use those exact words as we pray. But the words of that prayer are a perfect summary of what a servant of the Lord pleads for to qualify for the promise the Savior makes to all whom He calls: "And whoso receiveth you, there I will be also, for I will go before your face. I will be on your right hand and on your left, and my Spirit shall be in your hearts, and mine angels round about you, to bear you up" (D&C 84:88).

Think of that prayer as a standard of service. The prayer begins with reverence for our Heavenly Father. Then the Lord speaks of the kingdom and its coming. The servant with a testimony that this is the true Church of Jesus Christ feels joy in its progress and a desire to give his or her all to build it up.

The Savior Himself exemplified the standard set by these next words of the prayer: "Thy will be done, as in heaven, so in earth" (Luke 11:2). That was His prayer in the extremity of offering the Atonement for all mankind and all the world (see Matthew 26:42). The faithful servant prays that even the apparently smallest task will be done as God would have it done. It makes all the difference to work and to pray for His success more than for our own.

Then the Savior set for us this standard of personal purity: "And forgive us our sins; for we also forgive every one that is indebted to us. And lead us not into temptation; but deliver us from evil" (Luke 11:4). The strengthening we are to give those we watch over comes from the Savior. We and they must forgive to be forgiven by Him (see Matthew 6:14). We and they can hope to remain clean only with His protection and with the change in our hearts that His Atonement makes possible. We need that change to have the constant companionship of the Holy Ghost. Such a gift might seem too lofty and too distant for us and for those we serve. But a prophet of the Lord named Samuel called and anointed a young man named Saul. On that very day, Samuel promised Saul: "And the Spirit of the Lord will come upon thee, and thou shalt prophesy with them, and shalt be turned into another man" (1 Samuel 10:6).

That promise was fulfilled, not after many years or months or even days. Contemplate the account in 1 Samuel, the tenth chapter: "And it was so, that when he had turned his back to go from Samuel, God gave him another heart: and all those signs came to pass that day. And when they came thither to the hill, behold, a company of prophets met him; and the Spirit of God came upon him, and he prophesied among them" (1 Samuel 10:9–10).

You may have confidence in the Lord's service. The Savior will help you do what He has called you to do, be it for a time as a worker in the Church or forever as a parent. You may pray for help enough to do the work and know that it will come.

Now, a word to those who have issued those calls in the

Church. When you did, you conveyed the trust of the Lord. But He placed a trust with you as well. Just as those members were called to watch over and strengthen others, you were placed under the same obligation to watch over and strengthen them. If you issued the call and gave no training or did not watch to see that the training was enough, you failed them and the Lord. Even with that training, the path will become difficult for them. You know that, and so you must watch and listen to see when they need strengthening. You will give just enough help to strengthen their faith that the Lord is watching over them and over the people they serve and that they may turn with confidence to Him. To do that well, you must do a lot of praying yourself, for guidance and for them.

3   Finally, a word to those of us who are served by those who are newly called. Our opportunity and our obligation is the same as theirs. We are to watch and strengthen. And each of us has almost endless chances to do it. Every meeting you attend, every class, every activity will have someone doing something that to them is at the limit of their capacities, or maybe a little beyond. Most of us carry into those situations the attitudes we learn in the world, where we may be quick to notice inferior service. It is too easy to think, *In the Lord's true Church, our standard of performance should be higher than that.*

There is more than one way to help the Lord lift them to that standard. One is to express or show our displeasure. I've been the beneficiary of another way, the better way. I've sensed when I was not doing very well when I was speaking or teaching or leading in a meeting. Most people can tell when they are failing. I have been able to tell when I have not been doing well, and I've looked out and seen someone in the audience apparently not paying attention to me, with eyes closed. I've learned not to be irritated. And then they've opened their eyes and smiled at me, with a look of encouragement that was unmistakable. It was a look that said as clearly as if they had spoken to me: *I know the Lord will help you and lift you up. I'm praying for you.* I've been in settings where many people listening to me were doing that. And I was lifted beyond what I knew were my abilities, or at least what I had thought my abilities were. You could serve that way when you see people struggling in their service.

It will take a lot of praying, but you could watch and you could strengthen, even when your only call in the Church at that moment is to be a follower of Jesus Christ and your only tools are to pray and smile and encourage.

There is a miracle appearing in the Church. I see it as I travel back to nations after an absence of only a short time. The members and the leaders are changed. Just as Alma promised, their souls have been enlarged and their understanding enlightened and their minds expanded (see Alma 32:28, 34). They have served each other in faith in the Lord Jesus Christ. He has sent them the Holy Ghost as a companion in answer to fervent prayer. Their watching over and testifying and loving and helping each other has let the Lord give a miracle of growth in the hearts and capacities of humble sons and daughters of God.

— 20 —

DEBT MANAGEMENT

Sometimes it is helpful to remember how much we owe others for our progress through life. Yes, each of us has sacrificed to get to where we are, but families have added their contributions, and others have given help far beyond what may have been expected or required. Some of your benefactors may not even know you. Some may have briefly crossed your path, offered a blessing gladly and with faith, and then moved on.

Your problem is how to manage your debt rather than hope to erase it. You can't repay your benefactors. You could not ever find many of them, and they wouldn't take repayment if you offered it. But you can from this day forward act so that your debt will be steadily reduced.

Let me give you three rules for managing the debts of gratitude you have accumulated in your life. First, wherever you may labor in life, give more than you take. Second, whoever is around you in life, find someone to help. And, third, ask God to multiply the power of your efforts to give and to help.

From a talk given at Brigham Young University–Idaho commencement exercises, 27 April 2002.

1. Let me suggest some examples of how to do it, from what I have learned in my own life. In one of the first years when I was the president of Ricks College, a young man came to my office in the old Spori Building. He was dressed poorly and was ill at ease. School was about to start in the fall. He said that he was a convert to the Church, that he had arrived with just enough money for tuition and nothing else, and that he wanted my help.

My mind raced to think of what aid I could arrange for him. He had no money for food that day, no money for a place to stay, and no way to buy books. He was sleeping in his car. When I began to talk about what we could give him, he held up his hand to stop me. He said, "I just want to know the names of some people in town who might have some logs they want split for firewood." He had an axe in his car. He said that he could make his own way, thanks. I learned later that he split more wood than he was paid for at each place he found a job. I watched him over the years, sure that he would forever more than pay his own way. Like him, be more a giver than a taker, wherever you are.

2. During the years I was at Ricks College, we had a basketball player from Australia. He had played for his national team. I understand he held the record for the most points scored by an individual in a single Olympic game. He later played in the NBA. And yet I remember watching him one day after we'd had a large gathering in the gymnasium. The chairs were cleared and the basketball team was gathering for their practice. Over to the side of the floor I saw our star. He was working with another player, one of the obscure ones, one whom the coach didn't play much. He was showing him, over

and over, patiently, how to make a move with the ball. I remember now the admiration I felt for him. He was thinking of someone else more than himself. He was remembering who had helped him. He was trying to lift someone to where he was. Like him, look at those around you and find someone to help.

Finally, you will need faith to get the help of God so you can give when you want to take and to help others when you need help yourself. You will need it most when times are hardest. I have seen that miracle more than once. I remember going into the home of a faculty member. He had just learned that his son had been killed in an accident. He could only have known for a few minutes or at most an hour. Yet he greeted me smiling. He gave me comfort rather than taking comfort from me. And he had only concern for his other children, to help them see the hope of eternal life that was so plain to him.

Like him, plead with God to multiply your efforts to give and to help. He loves you and is all powerful. He will help you to give and to serve others, even when it seems nearly impossible.

Then you can rest assured that you have done your best to manage your debts of gratitude. But, of course, your debts will only grow, since God always blesses bountifully his grateful servants.

— 21 —

Gifts of Love

father once asked me to advise him about giving a Christmas gift to his daughter. He just couldn't decide whether or not to give this gift, or how to give it. His daughter was a college student. Her hectic life of school activities was made even harder because she didn't have a car. She begged rides, and she sometimes missed appointments. Her dad didn't have enough money for another car, at least not without some real sacrifice by his family. But he found a used car he might buy for her if he cut enough corners on the family budget. And then he wondered. He asked me: "Will that car really be good for her, or will it be a problem? I love her, and she really could use it, but do you think it will help her or spoil her?"

I didn't try to answer his question then, but I could sense his worry and sympathize with him. You ought to have sympathy for both givers and getters at Christmastime. One Christmas, my sons Matthew and John and I spent time at a toy store. Above us a red Santa Claus spun slowly as the sound of a mother whispering with clenched teeth floated

From a talk given at a Brigham Young University devotional, 16 December 1980.

over the stacks of toys to our aisle: "Don't tell me what your brother did to you. I saw *everything*. Do you want me to hit you right here in the store? Now you go outside and sit on that bench. And you stay there. And if you don't, I won't get you a thing." John and I shrugged and smiled at each other as we moved on, and I hummed inwardly, "'Tis the season to be jolly . . ."

Gift giving isn't easy. It's *hard* to give a gift with confidence. There are so many things that can go wrong. You wonder if the person on the other end will want it. My batting average on that is low. At least I think it is. You can't really tell what gets returned after Christmas, but I'm cautious enough that I always wrap the gift in the box from the store where I bought it.

I've always daydreamed of being a great gift giver. I picture people opening my gifts and showing with tears of joy and a smile that the giving, not just the gift, has touched their hearts. You must have that daydream, too. Many of you are probably already experts in gift giving. But even the experts may share some of my curiosity about what makes a gift great. I've been surrounded by expert gift givers all my life. None of them has ever told me how to do it, but I've been watching and I've been building a theory. I think it's finally ready to be shared. Here it is: The Eyring Theory of Gift Giving and Receiving. I call it a theory because it is surely incomplete. And calling it a theory means I expect you will change and improve it. I hope so, because then it will be yours. But at least I can help your theory building along.

My theory comes from thinking about many gifts and many holidays, but one day and one gift can illustrate it. The day was not Christmas or even close to it. It was a summer day. My mother had died in the early afternoon. My father, my brother, and I had been at the hospital. As we walked out, my brother and I went to the car together, smiled, and looked up at the mountains. We remembered how Mother had always said she loved the mountains so much. He and I laughed and guessed that if the celestial worlds are really flat, like a sea of glass, she would be eager to get away to build her own worlds, and the first thing she'd build would be mountains. With that we smiled and got into the car and drove home. We went to the family home, and Dad met us there. There were just the three of us.

Friends and family came and went. In a lull, we fixed ourselves a snack. Then we visited with more callers. It grew late and dusk fell; I remember we still had not turned on the lights.

Then Dad answered the doorbell again. It was Aunt Catherine and Uncle Bill. When they'd walked just a few feet past the vestibule, Uncle Bill extended his hand, and I could see that he was holding a bottle of cherries. I can still see the deep red, almost purple, cherries and the shining gold cap on the mason jar. He said: "You might enjoy these. You probably haven't had dessert."

We hadn't. The three of us sat around the kitchen table and put some cherries in bowls and ate them as Uncle Bill and Aunt Catherine cleared some dishes. Uncle Bill then asked: "Are there people you haven't had time to call? Just give me some names, and I'll do it." We mentioned a few relatives who would want to know of Mother's death. And then Aunt

Catherine and Uncle Bill were gone. They could not have been with us more than twenty minutes.

Now, you can understand my theory best if you focus on one gift: the bottle of cherries. And let me explain this theory from the point of view of one person who received the gift: me. As we'll see, that is crucial. What matters in what the giver does is what the receiver feels. You may not believe that yet, but trust me for the moment. So let's start from inside me and with the gift of the bottle of cherries.

As nearly as I can tell, the giving and receiving of a great gift always has three parts. Here they are, illustrated by that gift on a summer evening.

First, I knew that Uncle Bill and Aunt Catherine had felt what I was feeling and had been touched. I'm not over the thrill of that yet. They must have felt we'd be too tired to fix much food. They must have felt that a bowl of home-canned cherries would make us, for a moment, feel like a family again. And not only did they feel what I felt; they were touched by it. Just knowing that someone had understood meant far more to me than the cherries themselves. I can't remember the taste of the cherries, but I remember that someone knew my heart and cared.

Second, I felt that the gift was free. I knew Uncle Bill and Aunt Catherine had chosen freely to bring a gift. I knew they weren't doing so to compel a response from us. At least to me, they seemed to receive joy from just giving their gift to us.

And third, there was sacrifice. Now you might say: "Wait. How could they give for the joy of it and yet make a sacrifice?" Well, I could *see* the sacrifice because the cherries were home bottled. That meant Aunt Catherine had prepared them for her family. They must have liked cherries. But she took that possible pleasure from them and gave it to us. That's sacrifice. However, since then I have realized this marvelous fact: It must have seemed to Uncle Bill and Aunt Catherine that they would have more pleasure if we had the cherries than if they did. There was sacrifice, but they made it for a greater return: our happiness. Most people feel deprived as they sacrifice to give another person a gift and then let that person know it. But only expert givers let the receiver sense that their sacrifice brings them joy.

Well, there it is—a simple theory. When you're on the receiving end, you will discover three things in great gift givers: they feel what you feel and are touched, they give freely, and they count sacrifice a bargain.

Now, it may not be easy to use this theory to make big strides in your gift giving. I don't expect you'll all rush out now and buy gifts brilliantly. It will take some practice—more than one holiday—to learn how to feel and be touched by what is inside someone else. And giving freely and counting sacrifice as joy will take a while. But you could start by being a good *receiver*. You might notice and you might appreciate. My theory suggests that you have the power to make others great gift givers by what you notice. You could make any gift better by what you choose to see. And you could, by failing to notice, make any gift a failure.

You can guess the advice I might have given my friend—the one with the carless daughter. Would a car be a good gift? Of course it could be, but something very special must happen in the eyes of that daughter. On Christmas morning, her eyes would need to see past the car to Dad and to the family.

If she saw that he had read her heart and really cared; if she saw that she had not wheedled the car from the family, and that they had not given it to extract some performance; and if she really saw the sacrifice and the joy with which it was made for her—then the gift would be more than wheels. In fact, the gift would still be carrying her long after the wheels no longer turned. Furthermore, her appreciation, if it lasted, would have made a great gift of whatever awaited her on that Christmas morning.

Gift giving requires both a sensitive giver and a sensitive receiver. I hope we will use this little theory, not to criticize the gifts that come our way this year, but to see how often our hearts are understood and gifts are given joyfully, even with sacrifice.

There is also something you could do to start becoming a better gift giver yourself. You could begin to put some gifts—great gifts—on layaway for the future.

I learned about this during a religion class I taught once at Ricks College. I was teaching from section 25 of the Doctrine and Covenants. In that section, Emma Smith is told that she should give her time to "writing, and to learning much" (D&C 25:8). As we read this verse together, I urged the class to be diligent in developing writing skills. But about three rows back sat a blonde girl whose brow wrinkled. She raised her hand and said: "That doesn't seem reasonable to me. All I'll ever write are letters to my children." That brought laughter all around the class. I felt chagrined to have applied that scripture to her. Just looking at her, I could imagine a full quiver of children around her. Maybe writing powerfully wouldn't matter to her.

Then a young man stood up near the back. He'd said little during the term; I'm not sure he'd ever spoken before. He was older than the other students, and he was shy. He asked if he could speak. He told in a quiet voice of having been a soldier in Vietnam. One day, in what he thought would be a lull, he had left his rifle and walked across his fortified compound to mail call. Just as he got a letter in his hand, he heard a bugle blowing, and shouts and mortar and rifle fire coming ahead of the swarming enemy. He fought his way back to his rifle, using his hands as weapons. Along with the other men who survived, he drove the enemy out. The wounded were evacuated. Then he sat down among the living, and some of the dead, and he opened his letter. It was from his mother. She wrote that she'd had a spiritual experience that assured her that he would live to come home if he would remain righteous. Recounting this experience to my class, the boy said quietly: "That letter was scripture to me. I kept it." And he sat down.

If you don't have a child now, you may have one someday, perhaps a son. Can you see his face? Can you see him somewhere, sometime, in mortal danger? Can you feel the fear in his heart? Does it touch you? Would you like to give freely? What sacrifice will it take to write the letter your heart will want to send? You won't do it in the hour before the postman comes. Nor will it be possible in a day or even in a week. It may take years. But you can start preparing now. It won't seem like sacrifice if you picture that boy, feel his heart, and think of the letters he'll need someday.

There is another gift some of you may want to give that will require starting early. I saw it started once when I was a bishop. A student sat across my desk from me. He talked about mistakes he had made. And he talked about how much he wanted his future children to have a dad who could use his priesthood—and to whom they could be sealed forever. He said he knew that the price and pain of repentance might be great. And then he said something I will not forget: "Bishop, I am coming back. I will do whatever it takes. I am coming back." He felt sorrow. And he had faith in Christ. And still it took months of painful effort.

But because he was willing to repent, somewhere this Christmas there is a family with a righteous priesthood bearer at its head. They have eternal hopes and peace on earth. He'll probably give his family all sorts of gifts wrapped brightly, but nothing will matter quite so much as the one he started a long time ago in my office and has never stopped giving. He felt then the needs of children he'd only dreamed of, and he gave early and freely. He sacrificed his pride and sloth and numbed feelings. I am sure it doesn't seem like sacrifice now.

He could give that gift because of other gifts given long ago. God the Father gave His Son, and Jesus Christ gave us the Atonement, the greatest of all gifts and all giving. They somehow felt all the pain and sorrow of sin that would fall on us and everyone else who would ever live. I testify that what Paul said is true:

"We have a great high priest, that is passed into the heavens, Jesus the Son of God. . . .

"For we have not an high priest which cannot be touched with the feeling of our infirmities; but was in all points tempted like as we are, yet without sin.

"Let us therefore come boldly unto the throne of grace, that we may obtain mercy, and find grace to help in time of need" (Hebrews 4:14–16).

I bear you my testimony that Jesus gave that gift freely, willingly, to us all. He said: "Therefore doth my Father love me, because I lay down my life, that I might take it again. No man taketh it from me, but I lay it down of myself" (John 10:17–18). All men and women come into this life with that gift. They will live again, and if they will, they may live with Him.

And I bear you testimony that as you accept that gift, given through infinite sacrifice, it brings joy to the giver. Jesus taught, "I say unto you, that . . . joy shall be in heaven over one sinner that repenteth, more than over ninety and nine just persons, which need no repentance" (Luke 15:7).

If that warms you as it does me, you may well want to give a gift to the Savior. Others did at His birth. Knowing what we know, how much more do we want to give Him something? But He seems to have everything. Well, not quite. He doesn't have you with Him again forever, not yet. I hope you are touched by the feelings of His heart enough to sense how much He wants to know you are coming home to Him. You can't give that gift to Him in one day, or one Christmas, but you could show Him today that you are on the way. You could pray. You could read a page of scripture. You could keep a commandment.

If you have already done these, there is still something left to give. All around you are people He loves but can help only through you and me. One of the sure signs that we have accepted the gift of the Savior's atonement is that we give gifts to others. The process of cleansing seems to make us more sensitive, more gracious, more pleased to share what means so much to us. I suppose that's why the Savior spoke of giving when He described those who would finally come home.

> Then shall the King say unto them on his right hand, Come, ye blessed of my Father, inherit the kingdom prepared for you from the foundation of the world:
>
> For I was an hungred, and ye gave me meat: I was thirsty, and ye gave me drink: I was a stranger, and ye took me in:
>
> Naked, and ye clothed me: I was sick, and ye visited me: I was in prison, and ye came unto me.
>
> Then shall the righteous answer him, saying, Lord, when saw we thee an hungred, and fed thee? or thirsty, and gave thee drink?
>
> When saw we thee a stranger, and took thee in? or naked, and clothed thee?
>
> Or when saw we thee sick, or in prison, and came unto thee?
>
> And the King shall answer and say unto them, Verily I say unto you, Inasmuch as ye have done it unto one of the least of these my brethren, ye have done it unto me. (Matthew 25:34–40.)

And that, I suppose, is the nicest effect of receiving great gifts. It makes us want to give, and give well. I've been blessed all my life by such gifts. I acknowledge that. I'm sure you do, too. Many of those gifts were given long ago. We're near the birthday of the Prophet Joseph Smith. He gave his great talent, and his life, that the gospel of Jesus Christ might be restored for me and for you. Ancestors of mine from Switzerland and Germany and Yorkshire and Wales left home and familiar ways to embrace the restored gospel, as much for me as for them, perhaps more. It was ten years after the Saints came into these mountains before my great-grandfather's journal shows one reference to so much as a Christmas meal. One entry reads, in its entirety: "December 25, 1855: Fixed a shed and went to the cedars. Four sheep died last night. Froze." I acknowledge such gifts, which I only hope I am capable of sending along to people I have not yet seen.

"Freely ye have received, freely give" (Matthew 10:8).

I pray that we will freely give. I pray that we will be touched by the feelings of others, that we will give without feelings of compulsion or expectation of gain, and that we will know that sacrifice is made sweet to us when we treasure the joy it brings to another heart.

INDEX